AN

INDIAN
WOMAN

IN

ISLAMABAD

1997-2000

ADVANCE PRAISE FOR THE BOOK

'Ruchi Ghanashyam was in Pakistan at an exciting time, when India and Pakistan fought a war, became overt nuclear weapon states, when Pakistan underwent a military coup, and when IC 814 was hijacked to Kandahar. Ghanashyam was an astute observer and participant in these events. In addition to the already onerous professional challenges that an Indian diplomat faces in Pakistan, and the exceptional circumstances of her posting, she had the further complexities of being a modern Indian woman in a traditional patriarchal society, with the demands of raising a family. It is only right that this deft and accessible book should bring to the general public what some of us in the foreign service have long known—the aplomb, yet modesty, with which the author dealt with these challenges and turned them into opportunities and served the national interest. This is a book to instruct diplomats, delight the general reader and inspire women of all ages'—Shivshankar Menon, former foreign secretary and national security adviser of India

'This is a memoir that brings life to the tangled complexities of a relationship between two neighbours who have remained adversaries throughout their history as independent nations. With skilled expertise, born of her years as a professional diplomat, Ruchi Ghanashyam weaves the tapestry of a life lived through various settings and scenarios in Pakistan. Her diplomatic tenure in Islamabad was witness to key, fundamental milestones in the relationship. This is more than a ringside view; it is a living history told with the skill of keen observation and profound insight. The fact that the writer served as an Indian woman diplomat navigating the daily challenges of her work in Pakistan, makes this fascinating story doubly compelling'—Nirupama Rao, former foreign secretary

'Ruchi Ghanashyam's tenure in Pakistan witnessed a pronounced see-saw in bilateral relations from the nuclear tests to Prime Minister Vajpayee's Lahore visit to the Kargil conflict to the Musharraf coup and then the IC 814 hijacking. This fascinating book covers the full interface of India–Pakistan relations, from the personal to the geopolitical, while exploring deeply rooted animosities and goodwill'—T.C.A. Raghavan, former Indian high commissioner to Pakistan and author

'Ruchi Ghanashyam's memoir offers a rare insight into one of the most complex bilateral relationships in modern diplomacy. As the first Indian woman diplomat posted to Islamabad, her unique perspective illuminates not only the geopolitical tensions of the late 1990s but also the subtle interplay of culture, gender and tradition in Pakistan. Beyond the high-stakes political arena, Ghanashyam's astute observations on Pakistani society and its potential for change demonstrate the depth of understanding that only immersive diplomacy can achieve'—Vikas Swarup, ex-diplomat and author

AN
INDIAN
WOMAN
IN
ISLAMABAD
1997-2000

RUCHI
GHANASHYAM

PENGUIN

VIKING

An imprint of Penguin Random House

PENGUIN VIKING

Penguin Viking is an imprint of the Penguin Random House group of companies whose addresses can be found at global.penguinrandomhouse.com

Published by Penguin Random House India Pvt. Ltd
4th Floor, Capital Tower 1, MG Road,
Gurugram 122 002, Haryana, India

Penguin
Random House
India

First published in Penguin Viking by Penguin Random House India 2024

ISBN 9780143466987

Typeset in Adobe Garamond Pro by Manipal Technologies Limited, Manipal
Printed at Replika Press Pvt. Ltd, India

www.penguin.co.in

To my father, who believed in me,
and to Ghanashyam, Anant and Aniket, for supporting me

Contents

1

Discovering Islamabad

It was not our choice to be the high commissioner's neighbours in Islamabad. My husband, A.R. Ghanashyam, and I had recently arrived, having been posted as counsellors at India's High Commission. We had two young boys, noisy and naughty as all schoolboys are. When the property agent took us to the house for the first time, we didn't even step inside. One really doesn't want to live next door to one's boss!

So, the property agents took us from house to house, one more unsuitable than the other. Some landlords were prejudiced against having Indian diplomats as tenants, fearing they might get into trouble with the authorities. Finally, after checking out more than a hundred properties, we found a suitable house with a willing landlord. He seemed keen to have us as tenants. A meeting was set up to secure a copy of the draft lease document. Just a couple of hours before the meeting, the prospective landlord called and expressed his regret as he wouldn't be able to rent his house to us. Nor could he provide any reasons.

We had recently arrived in Pakistan and were staying at the house earlier occupied by my predecessor. The lease of the house was available for a month. We, thus, had only that many days from the day of arrival to find another house.

We were starting to get nervous at the thought of soon being rendered homeless. The temporary accommodation was available for only a few more days. Our heavy, unaccompanied baggage, shipped from our previous posting, was stored in the living room. If we couldn't find a place to rent in a few days' time, we would need a place for ourselves and a storage space for our baggage. There seemed little room in government rules for such a situation and we certainly couldn't afford to stay at a hotel with our family of four and two domestic assistants for an indefinite period.

Our friends and colleagues kept reassuring us that we would find a place very soon, but nobody could really offer a solution. Only one of our colleagues was confident that we would soon find a place. He said presciently, 'Don't worry, the ISI [Inter-Services Intelligence] will lead you to the house they want you to live in.'

Sure enough, a few days later, we got a call from one of the property agents about a beautiful, large house with a big garden. The landlord was willing to rent it at much lower than its market value as it had been lying vacant for several months. The house had earlier been occupied by an ambassador and had undergone renovations thereafter.

We set out excitedly to see this mystery house. Lo and behold! It was the house next to the Indian High Commissioner's residence that we had turned down earlier. This time, however, we were more circumspect in our response. It was indeed large and beautiful, with six bedrooms, though a bit too large for us to maintain. The garden was large too, but out of shape. The landlord had converted the staff quarters in the backyard into a spacious flat that he could use when he visited Islamabad and had built a smaller staff quarter adjoining the house for the tenant. With no other option in hand, we agreed to talk. The rent for a house like that was obviously much higher than the rental ceiling for counsellors at the Mission. To our surprise, the agent didn't seem too perturbed. Before taking our leave, he promised to set up a meeting with his boss later that afternoon.

So, as per our discussion, we went to the property agent's office located on a first-floor office at the edge of Blue Market area of Islamabad. The owner of the agency was a tall, dark and large-built man with a thick beard. 'It's good that Ghanashyam has a beard these days,' I thought to myself. The owner of the agency also seemed to think so. He made an approving remark about Ghanashyam's beard, before asking him the reason why he had kept one. I was apprehensive of what the response might be as I knew that the beard was meant to save shaving time in the mornings. Fortunately, the nascent bond wasn't broken as the man replied to his own question, 'Perhaps you've grown the beard out of respect (*Ehtiram ke liye*),' he said with visible approval. I quickly agreed with his remark. Ghanashyam also nodded sagely!

The agent quoted a far more reasonable rent than what the Mission paid for the high commissioner's residence next door. But it was still too high for us and totally out of our reach. Had we not been desperate, we would not even have considered the proposal. But given our situation, we tried to negotiate. Ghanashyam applied his skills learnt at the Indian Institute of Management Ahmedabad. He argued that the landlord's apartment at the back severely compromised our privacy, especially as the drive went through the grounds of the house. Eventually, he brought them down to what seemed to be their lowest limit. This was still higher than our rental ceiling, though it was half of the rent paid for the house next door occupied by our high commissioner. We returned to the Mission somewhat downcast.

The Mission decided to make a reference to the government seeking enhancement of our rental ceiling. Considering that an indefinite stay at a hotel would have been an expensive proposition, the enhancement was quickly approved. I have often wondered if it was the financial angle or the amusement of our colleagues in the ministry at our plight of having to live next door to our boss with two noisy young boys that prompted the quick approval.

It appeared as though the Pakistani intelligence agencies had succeeded in guiding us to the house they appeared to have chosen for us! This suspicion was further strengthened when we learnt that the owner of the property agency had retired as a colonel from Pakistan's intelligence agency, ISI. At least, we finally had a house to move into!

The process of searching for a house was highly stressful and a time of deep anxiety. Our younger son got a nasty cut on his leg from an abandoned piece of broken glass. He had to be rushed to the nearest clinic to get stitches on the long and bleeding gash. His stitches were to be taken out the evening prior to our shifting but had to be postponed as I had to sit late in office to finish some work. Unfortunately, I was called to office again the next day while we were driving behind our luggage van. I had to spend the rest of the day more or less twiddling my thumbs restlessly at work while Ghanashyam managed the shifting.

A few weeks after moving into our new house, I received a panicky call from our domestic help. Some people had barged into our house and one of them was carrying a gun. They were led by a woman who claimed to be the owner of the house. They went all over the house, including the kitchen and our bedrooms, despite the protests of our staff. Their intentions were unclear, but the aggressive behaviour of the woman and the unfriendly gunman scared both our staff and our young children, who witnessed this intrusion. Thankfully, they never returned and we never found out the identity of the mystery intruders.

Having moved to our new home, we tried to settle down to a new life in Islamabad. A few months after shifting, we were surprised to hear a song from a popular Bollywood movie called *Border* being played on the loudspeaker at the corner of our street.

Border is based on the Battle of Longewala during the 1971 India–Pakistan War, where around 150 Indian soldiers defended their post throughout the night against a forceful assault by around 2000 Pakistani soldiers with armoured support. The unabashedly patriotic Indian film was banned in Pakistan. It was surreal to hear Sonu Nigam singing the popular Bollywood song '*Sandese aate hain*' in the heart of Islamabad. During our stay, we realized that despite restriction on screenings of Indian films,[1] not only was Bollywood extremely popular, but it was easy to find DVDs of Indian films at rental shops. We bought our own copy of *Border* in a market outside Peshawar.

A casual visitor to Islamabad could be forgiven for thinking of it as a prosperous city with wide streets and luxurious houses built on large plots of land besides tree-lined streets. A closer look would reveal the less fortunate, mainly Christian minorities, living in small neighbourhoods, hidden behind high walls. Many of them performed menial tasks, like sweeping the streets. There was one such neighbourhood at the beginning of our street. The song from *Border* was playing at the corner outside this colony.

In his first presidential address to the Constituent Assembly of Pakistan on 11 August 1947, Mohammed Ali Jinnah promised a secular Pakistan to all its minorities.[2] Pakistan never really became this promised land, with freedom and equality for all minorities.

---

[1] Indian films were banned by the military ruler General Ayub Khan in 1965, after the second India–Pakistan war. It took another military dictator, General Pervez Musharraf, to remove the ban on Indian films in 2007—more than forty years later. In August 2019, following India's removal of Article 370 of India's Constitution affecting Jammu and Kashmir, Indian films once again found themselves under the hammer.

[2] Shazia Hassan, 'Quaid's Aug 11 speech to be included in school curriculum', *Dawn*, 24 March 2015; Quoted extensively, including by Shahzeb Jillani, 'The search for Jinnah's vision of Pakistan', BBC News, 11 September 2013.

Pakistan's second prime minister, Khawaja Nazimuddin, is quoted as saying, 'I do not agree that religion is a private affair of the individual nor do I agree that in an Islamic state every citizen has identical rights, no matter what his caste, creed, or faith.'[3]

Pakistan has been a witness to repeated attacks on minority religious places and congregations and brutal killings of worshipers. Kidnappings, forcible conversion and marriage of minor Hindu and Sikh girls, attacks on Christian schools and places of worship, targeted killing of Shias and declaration of Ahmadis as non-Muslims, have all contributed to the insecurity felt by Pakistan's minorities.

Throughout our stay in Pakistan, we came across instances that highlighted the unequal status of Pakistan's minorities. Even the Shias were not spared. Several news reports covered stories of migration of prominent Shia professionals out of Pakistan due to targeted assassinations.[4]

As we started to settle down, we found that our new house had no display cabinet for our collection of Indian artefacts, and porcelain and crystal from different parts of Europe. A few years earlier, I had met a delegate from Pakistan at a SAARC (South Asian Association for Regional Cooperation) dinner. He had somewhat tactlessly claimed that there was a belief in Pakistan that Indians, especially Hindus, were stingy people and preferred saving for the future instead of living a good life, in the present. That in contrast, Pakistanis believed in living well. With this in mind, we began searching for a high-quality display cabinet to show off our collection of Indian and European pieces.

---

[3] Widely quoted, including by Madiha Arsalan, 'Growing Up in a Pakistan Where We Did Not Know Religious Vigilantism', *Friday Times*, 7 September 2023.

[4] 'A New Era of Sectarian Violence in Pakistan', 5 September 2022, International Crisis Group.

Our search took us to a furniture store run in a double-storied house not far from where we lived. The furniture store had a collection of high-quality furniture made with solid rosewood. The furniture stood out with its beautiful machine polish, bevelled glass, elegant designs and the concealed lights and mirrors that would enhance the contents. The furniture was accordingly expensive. We selected a couple of pieces. In typical South Asian style, I asked the owner if he had any discounts on the prices. The owner was a retired colonel from the ISI. We had not tried to hide our identity as Indian diplomats. He promptly agreed to give us a generous discount, saying, 'How can I not give you a discount? After all, you are our neighbours, even if you are quarrelsome neighbours (*jhagdalu padosee*)!'

Our search for a house had taken us to different parts of Islamabad. Moving around Islamabad was useful in understanding the geography of the city. Islamabad is a newly built town; it hasn't grown haphazardly over the years. Built only some decades back, it is well planned. Most of the city is laid out in grids set on either side of an arterial road. Each square in the grid is further divided into four subsections, with a small market at the centre. The sectors are numbered in a combination of letters and numbers and the subsections of each sector are numbered one to four and follow a set pattern. The house numbers also follow a regular pattern. Our house was in sector F7/2, that is, the second subsection of sector F7. The address was like a geographic coordinate, and once the layout of the city was understood, one could locate almost any address precisely without a map. In the absence of Google Maps, and no proper city map, the understanding of Islamabad's geography came in handy in the months that followed.

Islamabad wasn't the original capital of Pakistan. Karachi, the southern port city, was the provisional capital at the time of Pakistan's creation in 1947. Karachi's location was a major factor behind moving the capital. It was also filled with commercial and business activities. Being at the southern end of West Pakistan, Karachi was difficult to access from the rest of the western segment of the country, though the distance from East Pakistan (now Bangladesh) remained unaffected by the move. The location of Karachi on the Arabian Sea made it vulnerable to a naval assault. It was also at a distance from the army headquarters in Rawalpindi. The military ruler of Pakistan, General Ayub Khan, saw these as serious disadvantages and desired a new capital for Pakistan.

Everyone was not happy with General Khan's new venture. Sheikh Mujibur Rahman, the founder of Bangladesh, was reminded of the smell of the 'jute fields of Chittagong'[5] when he first visited the site of Islamabad. This was his way of comparing the paltry development effort in East Pakistan as compared to the rather generous amounts to be spent on the construction of the new capital. This sense of discrimination was also felt in the province of Balochistan.

A commission was constituted in 1958 to select a suitable site near Rawalpindi for Pakistan's new capital. The emphasis was on location, climate, logistics and defence requirements. After extensive search and examination of options, the commission identified the area north-east of Rawalpindi, at the base of the Margalla Hills. The new capital of Pakistan was constructed in the 1960s. The master plan of the city was designed by a Greek firm of architects, Doxiadis Associates, led by Constantinos Apostolou Doxiadis. General Khan apparently gazed over the empty patch, where the capital would come up, from the greenery of the hills of Shakarparian. It has, since, been developed into a park and recreational point with a panoramic view of Islamabad.

The movement of the capital from Karachi was a complicated exercise. At the time of the move, the new capital lacked markets

---

[5] Vaqas, 'Golden jubilee: From sleepy town to vibrant city, Islamabad turns 50', *Express Tribune*, 5 June 2012.

and even housing for the many bureaucrats. Schools, hospitals and other infrastructure was also inadequate. The capital was shifted temporarily to the garrison city of Rawalpindi in the early 1960s, and then to Islamabad when essential development work was completed in 1966. People would often tell us that most offices had to be temporarily housed in what is now Fatima Jinnah Women University.

Almost three decades after becoming the capital, Islamabad remained a small, sleepy and dull town. One heard that at its inception, Islamabad was often light-heartedly described as 'half the size of Arlington Cemetery (of Washington, DC) and twice as dead'. Despite a population of over half a million (without Rawalpindi), in the late 1990s, diplomats continued to describe it in the same words.

There was virtually no public transport system; locals coming to work in Islamabad from the nearby villages were compelled to either walk or use overcrowded private minibuses. The entertainment scene did not fare better, the city had only one cinema and it normally screened Pakistani or other out-of-date movies. There were virtually no good sports facilities in the city, though the Islamabad Club offered some dining and sports facilities. The club had a swimming pool, with different timings for men and women, thereby ruling out a family outing to the pool. The golf course was a welcome diversion for those who liked playing the game. We preferred the privacy afforded by the American Embassy Club as it kept our 'minders' from the Pakistani intelligence out. The restaurant at the Club served an excellent cuisine and it had good facilities, including a gym, swimming pool, and spacious grounds for children to play baseball and basketball. I spent many Saturdays on the benches reading the weekend papers while our children played sports with other children. The American Embassy Club was really the only place in Islamabad where we felt like normal people, living normal lives.

A year or so into our posting, we were invited for a party by the owner of the moving company that had handled our baggage. It was rumoured that he was one of the few people 'cleared' by the intelligence agencies to invite Indians to his home. His company was on our High Commission's approved panel of packers and entertaining us could be seen as business promotion. While talking to him during the dinner, I expressed my appreciation for the well-laid-out plan of Islamabad. I added that the grid-like layout made it easy to understand the geography of the city and to locate an address; we had understood the layout of the city while searching for a house. His response stunned me: 'Now you see why we have to follow you everywhere; you understood our city's geography while searching for your house. If we let you be, there's no guessing what else you might figure out.' Perhaps this explained the underlying paranoia of the Pakistani establishment and the extreme measures they took to keep a tab on everything we did.

Though Islamabad was a dull place, it had its diversions. One of these was the historical ruins of the ancient Indian city of Taxila, situated around 30 km from Islamabad. Apart from the Mauryan and Kushan empires, the ruins provide interesting insights into the Indo-Greek and Indo-Scythian periods. Taxila reached its apogee between the first and fifth centuries and is considered one of the most important archaeological sites in Asia. Rediscovered by renowned archaeologist Sir Alexander Cunningham in the mid-nineteenth century and included in the UNESCO World Heritage site list in 1980, Taxila was one of the major tourist attractions of Pakistan. It is here that one of the world's earliest universities flourished, where Vishnugupta, better known as Chanakya or Kautilya, was a scholar. The renowned strategist Chanakya guided Chandragupta Maurya to the throne of Magadh, with its capital in Patliputra.[6] Chandragupta went on to establish a pan-Indian empire in ancient India, the Mauryan

---

[6] Pataliputra: Modern Patna, capital of Bihar state in eastern India.

Empire. Chanakya's landmark work, *Arthashastra*,[7] the world's first written guide on diplomacy and the science of politics, is believed to have been composed at Taxila, which is also said to have hosted the ancient Ayurvedic healer Charaka, first as a student and then as a tutor. Panini, the grammarian who codified the rules of classical Sanskrit, is understood to have been a part of the Taxila community.

Notwithstanding its enormous significance, Taxila was not very well preserved in those days, despite the devoted efforts of Prof. Ahmad Hasan Dani, renowned archaeologist, historian and linguist. Prof. Dani was the first Muslim to graduate from Banaras Hindu University in 1944 with a master's in Sanskrit.[8] Taxila's neglect was highlighted in the 2012 report of the Global Heritage Fund,[9] which listed it among the ten world sites that were most in danger of irreparable loss and damage. Subsequent preservation efforts are reported to have helped preserve this global heritage site. Visits to Taxila were one of the rare privileges of living in Islamabad and remain a treasured memory.

Another attraction was Panja Sahib, about an hour's drive from Islamabad in the town of Hasan Abdal. The imprint of the *panja* (right hand) of Guru Nanak, the founder of the Sikh religion, is preserved on a rock in the shrine of Panja Sahib. To the faithful Sikhs, Panja Sahib is one of the holiest shrines of their religion and is held in high esteem. Every year, thousands of Sikh pilgrims from all over the world converge at Panja Sahib.

Rawalpindi, or Pindi, as it was popularly called, was good for a special outing. Hundreds of small shops sold a variety of dress

[7] 'Arthashastra' literally means 'Treatise on Economics' but covers varied subjects, from nature of government, law, markets and trade, diplomacy, theories on war and nature of peace, to duties and obligations of a king.

[8] Lawrence Joffe, 'Ahmad Hasan Dani', *Guardian*, 31 March 2009.

[9] Global Heritage Fund, 'Saving Our Vanishing Heritage: Asia's Heritage in Peril', May 2012.

materials, mostly brought from China. Designer prints on silk, commissioned by famous Italian designers, fabricated in China, found their way to the markets in Peshawar, Pindi and Lahore and were sold at unbelievably low prices. One of the shopkeepers in Pindi explained that factories in China could discard a certain percentage of their production as defective. This was bought by Pakistani traders. Some of the Chinese fabrics were printed in Pakistan itself. In the absence of other diversions, one could blow away the blues by shopping in the by-lanes of Pindi.

Rawalpindi is Pakistan's fourth largest city and is considered a twin city of Islamabad. It became a major city under the Sikh Empire, and a garrison town of the British following its conquest in 1849. After the partition of India in 1947, it was the capital of Pakistan from 1959 to 1969 and became the headquarters of the Pakistan Army. True power in Pakistan is believed to reside in Rawalpindi rather than in Islamabad, no matter who rules Pakistan.

The mountain resort town of Murree, on the outskirts of Islamabad, about 30 km away in the Pir Panjal Range, was another pleasant diversion. Murree is believed by some to be the final resting place of Mother Mary or Maryam, hence the name. The town has the dubious distinction of having hosted former prime minister Zulfikar Ali Bhutto at the Government House following the military coup by General Mohammad Zia-ul-Haq. It is here that Bhutto met Zia ten days after the coup and supposedly reminded Zia of Article 6 of Pakistan's Constitution, according to which the coup was tantamount to high treason.[10] Many consider it as the reason behind Bhutto's eventual arrest and hanging.

---

[10] Article 6: High treason

1. Any person who abrogates or subverts or suspends or holds in abeyance, or attempts or conspires to abrogate or subvert or suspend or hold in abeyance, the Constitution by use of force or show of force or by any other unconstitutional means shall be guilty of high treason.

The High Commission had a small guest house in Murree with a caretaker, and on the rare occasion, one could visit it over the weekend to relax, away from the pressure of living under almost constant watch in Islamabad. A popular tourist destination, Murree had been built as a sanatorium for British soldiers. It was on one such visit to Murree that I had a memorable exchange with a Pakistani shopkeeper. He refused to accept that I was a foreigner in Pakistan. He was convinced that if not a current resident of Karachi, I had 'drunk its water' sometime. My colleague's wife and my close friend, Abha, and I, both spoke to him in chaste Hindustani, with the occasional use of Urdu words and phrases preferred by people in Pakistan. With so much similarity at the people-to-people level, the distance between the establishments sometimes caused us a twinge of sadness.

Living in Islamabad was not easy. One was constantly under pressure of daily, non-stop surveillance. One had to presume that the house and telephone were bugged. The town itself offered little diversion and one needed official permission to go out of city limits. The permission wasn't always forthcoming. Rawalpindi town and Murree were the exceptions and could be visited without prior permission of the Foreign Office. Formal clearance was required for visits to all other places. We were denied permission to go on a group heritage tour to Khyber Pass. Worse still, our nine years old, elementary school-going younger son was denied permission to go on a class field trip with a visiting American

---

2. Any person aiding or abetting or collaborating the acts mentioned in clause (1) shall likewise be guilty of high treason.

2A. An act of high treason mentioned in clause (1) or clause (2) shall not be validated by any court including the Supreme Court and a High Court.

3. Majlis-e-Shoora (Parliament) shall by law provide for the punishment of persons found guilty of high treason.

expert to learn about stalactites at the Khewra Salt Mines, 150 km from Islamabad.

Upon my return from Islamabad to Delhi, I was posted as director (Pakistan) in the Ministry of External Affairs. A year or so into the job, my counterpart from the Pakistan Mission came to see me to convey that the Pakistan Foreign Office had decided to restrict the movement of our High Commission's personnel to the city limits of Islamabad. The Pakistani decision to restrict our officials in Islamabad to an area no larger than a section of south Delhi, was unacceptable. I told my counterpart that if our staff was restricted to Islamabad alone, we would reciprocate by restricting Pakistan High Commission officials to New Delhi Municipal Council area where Pakistan High Commission and South Block, home to India's Foreign Office, are located. He immediately objected as some of their officers lived outside this area. Instinctively, I responded firmly that they could either move those officers to the NDMC area or seek our permission for their to-and-fro movement on a daily basis. I was greatly relieved to learn subsequently that the Pakistan Foreign Office had changed its mind on this issue and that for the time being, our officials posted in Islamabad and their families could continue to occasionally breathe the air outside the tiny Islamabad.

2

The Constant Shadows

'Let's go to the insurance company today on our way back to office from lunch,' I said to Ghanashyam on the office intercom. Understandably, he asked, 'Why do we have to go there?' 'I think the windshield of my car is about to be smashed. I just want to be sure that the insurance will cover it,' I responded.

Pakistani intelligence agents had been tailing us from the first day of arrival in Islamabad. Some months back, the agent tailing me had been changed. Unlike other agents, this one had a bold look about him. He often tried to strike a conversation. He would hang around when I got out of the car to open or close the gate of the house and would often pass comments like 'Mashallah'. I found his behaviour objectionable but tried to ignore him. Then, he started following me inside shops. On one occasion, we went in to buy some cosmetics. I found a nice face brush. Ghanashyam wanted to know what it was. I held it up playfully as if to apply powder on his face. But before I could do anything, my eyes landed on the agent just a few paces away, smiling knowingly at our domestic bliss!

One evening, I got a call from my friend Nusrat to come and visit her in her office on my way home. Nusrat was head of the Islamabad branch of the French bank Societe Generale. She was honoured with Chevalier d'Ordre National du Merite and was conferred with French citizenship.

As I left the Mission, the Pakistani agent followed me as usual, except that he had a partner with him. I parked my car across the street outside the multi-storey building where the bank's offices were located on the third floor. It was after office hours. The lift was closed, and the building was silent and somewhat dark. As I climbed the stairs, I noticed that the two Pakistani agents had crossed the street to follow me into the building, as against their normal practice of waiting outside. The sight of two tall and well-built Pakistani agents, wearing identical black trousers and black leather jackets, following me into a deserted building was unnerving and intimidating. On the second floor, I tried to open the door to get into Nusrat's office but found it to be locked. I rattled the door forcefully when I heard the footsteps of the two men coming closer. As panic began to rise inside me, I could feel perspiration on my face, perhaps the one time I felt real fear in Islamabad. The two agents came to the dark and narrow landing where I was standing but went up without saying a word. I calmed down a bit and realized that I had been banging on the wrong door and had to go up another floor for Nusrat's office. The incident infuriated me and left me somewhat shaken.

For some reason, it did not occur to me to complain to the Mission, either to the high commissioner or to our security chief. Being the first lady diplomat posted to the High Commission of India in Islamabad, perhaps, I did not want to show any signs of weakness.

Shortly thereafter, I met the director (India) in the Pakistan Foreign Office on 1 January to hand over the list of India's nuclear installations and facilities. This practice was put in place by the terms of the 'Agreement on the Prohibition of Attack against Nuclear Installations and Facilities between India and Pakistan'. It was signed as a confidence-building measure on 31 December 1988 (entered into force on 27 January 1991). Among its provisions is an agreement that India and Pakistan will inform each other of the nuclear installations and facilities to be covered under the Agreement on the first of January of every calendar year. The lists are exchanged through diplomatic channels at New Delhi and Islamabad. As counsellor (Political) in India's Mission in Islamabad, I went to the Ministry of Foreign Affairs of Pakistan to hand over India's list. Coincidentally, a couple of years later, I received the same list in South Block as the director (Pakistan) from the Pakistani officer to whom I had just handed over the Indian list in Islamabad.

Once the official part of the meeting was done, I spontaneously complained to him about the behaviour of their agent tailing me. He did not seem surprised or perturbed. Rather, he responded saying, 'But then you also go gallivanting all over the place; you seem to have too many friends!' I was furious at this comment and responded sharply that I was unlikely to be intimidated by such tactics, 'Had I been such a coward, I would not have opted for a posting to Islamabad. In India, girls handle such characters on public transport almost daily!'

The exchange with the director (India) had no impact on the situation and the attempted intimidation by the Pakistani agent continued. A few weeks later, I came to Delhi on 'Bag Duty'. Given the level of distrust in the bilateral relationship, the diplomatic bag was carried by hand between Islamabad and Delhi by the Mission's diplomatic officers on rotation on Bag Duty. The diplomatic immunity of the officer prevented the Pakistani customs authorities from opening the bags. While in South Block to collect the diplomatic bag from Delhi to Islamabad, I went to see Vivek Katju, the then joint secretary heading the desk dealing with Iran, Pakistan and Afghanistan. I told him about the harassment I was being subjected to in Islamabad. He was furious and immediately spoke to Pakistan's deputy high commissioner in Delhi. He reminded him in stark language that two could play at the game. Katju's message was loud and clear. India did not believe in or support any escalation of negativity. He conveyed to the Pakistani diplomat that, until then, ladies had been kept outside the cycle of harassment. He added that Pakistan was starting a new practice through such harassment of a lady officer, which could have serious repercussions. With this stern message, we hoped that the Pakistanis would step back.

A few days later, the day I asked Ghanashyam about the car insurance, I received a phone call from the director (India). Apparently, the Pakistani lady officer in Delhi had handed over her car for valet parking at a five-star hotel. While she was having dinner, a red Maruti van drove in and parked next to her car in the basement parking of the hotel. A couple of men with hockey sticks came out of the van, smashed the windshield of her car and drove away. Though I had no idea of the attack and had heard of it for the first time, the director (India) practically accused me of having instigated the incident. He clearly didn't believe my sincere denial. I didn't blame him. Had the situation been reversed, I too would not have believed him.

So, we went to the office of the insurance company to reassure ourselves that everything was in order and waited for the Pakistani retaliation. Surprisingly, there was none. There has never been any explanation for the lack of retaliation that we were expecting. A possible reason that comes to mind as a likely explanation is that the Pakistani establishment decided to step back, perhaps at a signal from the Pakistani foreign office, as the harassment had been started from their side.

Several months later, I was reminded of this incident at the Wagah/Attari Border between India and Pakistan. We were driving from Islamabad to Delhi with the children. As we waited for the completion of formalities on the Indian side of the border, we started a conversation with one of the soldiers on duty. He spoke of the stories they heard periodically of harassment of Indian officers in Islamabad, adding, 'You can imagine how our entire body burns with anger when we hear such stories. For us, the earth shakes when our officers walk on it.' I realized that reports of harassment of an Indian lady officer in Islamabad would have caused deep anguish to many people back home. My subdued and low-key reaction to harassment in Islamabad probably saved a lot of angst to people back home.

Pakistani agencies tried different tactics periodically to try and intimidate us on the road. One common tactic was aggressive driving. I too was subjected to it on occasions when driving alone. The tailing car would drive close to the bumper, increasing the speed or slowing down in response to my speed. They would also drive right beside as if about to overtake but would match my speed to stay parallel. An agent in the other car's passenger seat would constantly keep looking at me, smirking or even laughing at my discomfort. Blocking a car between two cars was another intimidatory technique that they tried occasionally with some officers, though I was spared.

People would often say, 'These are reciprocal tactics. India does the same to Pakistani diplomats in Delhi.' This is not true. For one thing, Delhi traffic does not allow for these games. Anyone trying these tricks in Delhi would face loud horns or worse from angry Indian drivers! Quite unlike Islamabad's wide and empty boulevards.

It was a visit to Karachi that probably represents the pinnacle of tailing as far as I am concerned. I was invited for tea by Husain Haqqani. A journalist, academic, political activist and former ambassador of Pakistan to Sri Lanka, he had been adviser to both Benazir Bhutto and Nawaz Sharif and was later Pakistan's ambassador to the US. Seven people tailed my car as we drove to his house, five of them in a car and two on a motorcycle. As he received me, Husain instructed his staff to offer tea to the agents who had accompanied me. I remember telling him that I was a more expensive guest than he had bargained for, 'I brought seven guests, apart from myself.'

At times, it seemed that the children were also not out of bounds. The High Commission ran Hindi classes for our school-going children. An office mini-van would pick up the children to take them to their classes. One afternoon, a car accompanied this van and the agents in the car tried to take a video of the children inside. An adult who was in the van told the children to duck below the windows to prevent the video from being made. Our little son was particularly traumatized by this experience.

The staff of the Mission were regular targets. They were 'picked up' periodically by Pakistani intelligence. At times, when the situation was tense and it seemed likely that the Pakistanis would try and pick up one of our staff, an assorted group that apprehended the danger would stay in the Mission premises for a few days until the danger passed. The Mission would deploy a bus to pick up and drop staff members. Often such periods of insecurity ended with someone being 'picked up'.

Late one afternoon, an agitated Lakhan, the Mission's gardener, entered my office. I was then working as the head of chancery, a glorified designation for the officer handling all administrative and establishment matters of the Mission. Lakhan was on the verge of breaking down and all he could convey was that he wanted to return home to India. It took a few minutes before he could calm down and narrate what was bothering him.

Lakhan had just returned from the custody of Pakistani intelligence. He had been 'picked up' as he was walking to the Mission and had been questioned about who was doing what at the Mission. Being a gardener, he worked outside the office building. In a Mission with over a hundred people, he was not even sure of the names of most of the staff, let alone where their office was located. His questioners were particularly interested in the identity of the people working in a specific section of the building that he never visited being the gardener. This must have become apparent to his questioners who let him go. The experience left him shaken as his daily walk to work had suddenly started looking like a dangerous adventure. He, therefore, wanted to be repatriated home at once.

Sending him back to India was not an option. It smacked of weakness and could only invite more frequent incidents of people being picked up. I tried to boost his morale and talked of the brave Indian soldiers who faced the enemy on the borders every day without fear. But no matter what I said, Lakhan remained adamant that he wanted to return to India.

When nothing else seemed to work, I got out of my office and asked him to accompany me. Outside the Mission's boundary wall, we maintained a wide patch of garden. It kept the front of the Mission attractive, while ensuring that intruders (or worse) stayed at a safe distance from the boundary wall. A group of Pakistani intelligence personnel sat opposite the corner of our property, on the other side of the road. As and when an officer left the Mission, one of them would take his motorcycle or car and follow. I took Lakhan to the same corner and stood there examining the plantation at the end of the property, just across the narrow street where the group of Pakistani intelligence personnel were sitting. We discussed the options for making that corner more attractive as if that was the most vital part of our garden. We returned to the Mission when he seemed reassured and confident once again. Lakhan completed his tenure and returned to serve a second term as gardener at the Mission in Islamabad.

It seemed sometimes that the purpose of the aggressive Pakistani tailing was to deter Pakistanis from getting friendly with us, more than to keep a watch on us. Sometimes though, the behaviour seemed inspired by malice. We had organized a week-long film festival for the fiftieth anniversary of India's independence at the small auditorium of the High Commission. The subtitled movies received from the Ministry of External Affairs included titles likely to appeal to a Pakistani audience from a cultural perspective. No politically inappropriate movie was in the list. The guest list for the festival included Pakistanis. A small reception was hosted each evening before the screening. There was enthusiastic response to the high commissioner's invitation. Most people who were invited, confirmed and we were worried that the audience may overflow our small auditorium.

The opening night had a big turnout. Several enthusiastic lovers of Bollywood joined the event. There was a large vacant piece of land opposite the High Commission. It had been acquired by our government for constructing a residential complex, but the project had been held up for years in the labyrinthine bureaucracy of Pakistan. We had no leverage, as Pakistan had already constructed its own residential complex in Delhi's diplomatic enclave in Chanakyapuri. I was slowly trying to unknot this gordian knot, but at that point, the land was lying vacant and was used occasionally for parking by guests of the High Commission. On this occasion, the cars were parked deep into the open land.

Soon after the event began, some Pakistani agents came and went around noting the car numbers. A few people were questioned too. The turnout was a bit lower on the second and third day, until on the last day there were just a handful of diplomats attending the event. Others had all been 'contacted'. The Press Trust of India and *The Hindu* newspaper had reporters based in Islamabad. One of them came by taxi and was stopped and questioned before he reached the building. Unfortunately for the intelligence personnel, they mistook him for a Pakistani, and we received a blow-by-blow account of his questioning by the agents. It would have taken a diehard Bollywood fan, with a lot of connections, to return to the Indian event after that kind of questioning.

Though Pakistan made a big deal about the treatment of its diplomats in Delhi, the atmosphere in the two countries was completely different. On my return from Islamabad, I was appointed director (Pakistan) in the Ministry of External Affairs. Around this time, our mission in Islamabad started complaining to me about the treatment of Sujit Kumar, our counsellor dealing with visas and consular matters. The Internet at his house was cut off and was not restored, despite several attempts. The lower-level staff at the telephone department in Islamabad simply put up their hands that they had 'instructions'! Sujit's children were unable to do their school assignments and homework which was posted on the Internet. The agents watching him also started peeping into his house through the fence, causing harassment to his teenage daughter. The Mission's complaints were bouncing off a stone wall. I tried to intercede with the Pakistani Mission in Delhi but to no avail.

I felt that the only way out was a tit-for-tat response. I had no idea how to get someone's Internet disconnected in Delhi. I finally found a senior officer of the telephone department of the area where Sujit's visa counterpart lived in Delhi. I had a hard time explaining to him that I was not in-charge of Pakistan, but just the director of the desk dealing with the country in the ministry in Delhi; and that I wanted someone's telephone line cut and not installed. It eventually dawned on him that he would be helping his own officer in Islamabad by cutting off the connection in Delhi. As a one-time exception, he agreed to do it. Before the end of the day, however, the connection was restored on a complaint by the Pakistani Mission. My purpose was served just by the brief disconnection; the Internet in Sujit's house was immediately restored. There is no official meddling by other departments in the day-to-day functioning of the telephone companies in India, several of which are in the private sector. Though it may not always be efficient, the system is streamlined in India; complaints are attended to as a matter of course.

It was not a frightening experience all the time, though. Islamabad was the only place where ordinary souls like us could feel a bit like James Bond. At times, I would try and drive into the side lanes to shake off the 'tail' or race the car to the next turning to try and disappear before they could catch up. I rarely succeeded. The roads in Islamabad often had no traffic and the agents could see which way the car had turned, even from a long distance. I managed to shake off my tail only on one occasion, when I was going to a tailor's shop in a market that I did not normally frequent. The triumphant feeling didn't last very long as five minutes later, the agents reached the market and parked at a short distance from my car. I was left wondering if the Pakistani agencies had such an efficient network across the city that they could trace our whereabouts in minutes!

The presence of the agents came in handy at times. My friends in India would often advise me not to drive around too much in Islamabad. My stock answer used to be, 'Don't worry, there's always someone driving behind. They would have to help me change the tyre in case I get a flat tyre'.

Once in Lahore, our children wanted to eat pizza at Pizza Hut, but the franchise didn't have a branch in Islamabad those days. We found the address and got the directions, but without a GPS, we were soon lost and driving around in circles. Finally, the agents driving behind us drove up to our car and asked Ghanashyam in desperation, '*Sir, aapko jaana kahan hai?*' (Sir, where do you want to go?) Our roles were then reversed, and we followed them to the restaurant. We got lost in Islamabad too, one night and the agents following us guided us quietly to our destination.

The presence of the agents behind us turned out to be useful in Karachi once. Ghanashyam was extremely popular with the business community in Karachi, many of whom were Bohra Muslims, originally from Mumbai and Gujarat. They were happy to meet us when we went to Karachi and talk about 'apna gaon' (back home). We had taken a big carton of gifts for friends in Karachi, discarding the carton soon after reaching the hotel. We didn't bargain for the Pakistani generosity and had no place for the return gifts in our small suitcase. When it was time to leave, we needed another bag! Karachi is a typical South Asian city with heavy traffic. Travel time is increased by one-way lanes. Our flight was in a few hours. I asked the driver to take me to the nearest baggage shop. Knowing our departure plans, he took the shortest way to the nearest market, until we reached a point beyond which the road was 'one way'. A traffic policeman was posted there. The driver was confident and aggressive enough to blow the horn persistently. Finally, the cop came over to the driver and angrily told him to move back. The driver quietly pointed backwards. The cop was suddenly transformed upon seeing the car following us, filled with agents in plain-clothes. He quickly went to the circle, stopped the traffic and gestured for us to go. But for that, we would probably have missed our flight that day!

At times, these situations turned comic. One such occasion was during a visit to Lahore. We were both accompanying High Commissioner G. Parthasarathy and his wife on their official visit to Lahore. The head of our consular and visa wing was also part of the team. One evening, we all had independent programmes as Parthasarathy and his wife had a private invitation. We left the hotel in our separate cars for our respective engagements. The next morning, I came out of the hotel door to call the cars to the porch to go for a meeting. I was surprised to see a familiar-looking man sidle up to me and ask about our counsellor (Visa), 'Madam, kal raat Behari sahab kahan gaye the?' (Madam, where did Mr Behari go last night?) I asked him wickedly, 'Why? Did you people lose him last night?' He confessed that their car had stalled at a traffic light and by the time they managed to turn the corner, Mr Behari's car had disappeared. As Mr Behari was driving himself, there was no driver to talk to! The agent needed to file a report about the place of visit, and dared not make a fake entry, in case someone else reported Mr Behari's presence elsewhere.

The treatment of Indian diplomats in Islamabad was sui generis. One can't think of another place in those days where Indian diplomats received such attention from the host state and its intelligence outfits or where they faced the risks they did in Islamabad. We had no privacy as the Pakistani agencies listened in to our phone calls and kept a close eye on what we did, where we went or whom we met. We had developed our own little codes for phone conversations. Sometimes, we would fix specific words to tie up our programme later. Other times, we used incorrect timings for our programme over the telephone. The intelligence agents followed specific duty hours. On rare occasions, we would fix our programme on the telephone but leave earlier than planned, just to have a little privacy with our families.

Even the waiters that we called to serve at our gatherings came wearing 'wires'! On one occasion, the wire slipped out of the waiter's sleeve as he was serving the guests.

Despite signing a 'Code of Conduct for treatment of diplomatic/consular personnel in India and Pakistan',[1] way back in 1992, Indian diplomats continued to face harassment and violence in pursuit of their official work. This 'Code of Conduct', I was told, was signed following an assault on a forty-five-year-old Indian police officer, who was forcibly taken away from his home as his protesting father was held back by Pakistani agents. According to reports, he was blindfolded while being taken for interrogation

---

[1] Signed on 19 August 1992, by J.N. Dixit and Shaharyar M. Khan, foreign secretaries of India and Pakistan, respectively.

and subjected to electric shocks and vicious blows. Each one of us in the Mission had heard the story of his mistreatment.

During our stay, people were regularly picked up and ill-treated. Dorab, who processed newspaper bills and handled routine files, was taken one day. On his return, he conveyed that he had been made to stand with his face to the wall, arms held up and brutally beaten with a rubber bat. There was little visible injury but for weeks he was unable to sleep on his back or sit in a chair and work. On one occasion the agencies 'picked up' Prem, an elderly assistant in the Mission. Our frantic efforts to intercede with the Pakistan foreign office were summarily rebuffed. Coincidentally, a couple of staff members of the Pakistani Mission became uncontactable for a few hours in Delhi the same evening during a shopping trip. Perhaps, the apprehension that they may have been picked up by Indian agencies prompted the quick release of Prem from the Pakistani custody. Prem said later that he had prepared himself for the torture. The agents left the room, apparently intending to return shortly. However, upon return, they just let him go. This probably saved his life; he was elderly and suffered from high blood pressure and diabetes and did not have any of his prescribed medicines with him. Such incidents happened at regular intervals.

Though we laughed, and at times, tried to shake off the tails playfully, the ugly reality was never far from our minds. A nagging sense of anxiety and insecurity was a part of our daily lives. It took a long time after returning to Delhi for us to stop looking over the shoulder for our 'shadows'.

3

Friendships amidst Suspicion

'Oh! It's so lovely to meet you! My family migrated to Karachi from India. We would really like you to visit our home and have dinner with us whenever you're free,' said the nice lady I had just met at a reception hosted by a business contact. She seemed to be from an affluent background, but I had never seen her before at any diplomatic events. She also missed the aura of the 'well-connected' Pakistani who could meet Indian diplomats with impunity. As she gushed about her family's links with and affection for India, I decided to be kind to her, 'You know that we don't come alone?' She obviously didn't understand me, so I explained to her that a representative of Pakistan's intelligence agencies always accompanied us wherever we went and sometimes our hosts received a follow-up visit from them. Not surprisingly, we never heard from her again.

The visible presence of the agencies following us deterred many friendships. We too hesitated at times from pursuing relationships to avoid unreasonable pressure on well-meaning

Pakistanis. Despite this handicap, some of our friendships from Islamabad have lasted for over two decades.

In the absence of other diversions, shopping for clothes and occasionally for jewellery and Afghan carpets kept most foreign women busy in Islamabad. Pakistani markets were filled with different varieties of fabrics in a wide range of prices. There were several excellent tailors and designers in Islamabad. As women in casual Western clothing attracted unnecessary and unwelcome attention, many women preferred to wear salwar-kameez and spent a lot of time getting them made.

My friend Nusrat was a wonderful shopping companion. One day, she tempted me with Pakistani chikan embroidery on chiffon fabric but said that we would have to travel in her car. I met her at a predetermined spot somehow managing to evade the 'shadows'. Between our home and hers was a large Naval Colony that was out of bounds for us. I had obviously never entered the colony. To my surprise, she nonchalantly turned her car into the Naval colony!

'Where are we going, Nusrat?' I asked her somewhat apprehensively. She explained that the Naval Colony market had received a new supply of exquisite Pakistani chikan from Bahawalpur, famous for its chikan work in Pakistan. I got worried as entry of Indian diplomats in defence areas was prohibited in Pakistan. 'If we get apprehended, I will be deported for spying, but you may be accused of treason,' I told her with fear in my voice. It turned out to be a worthwhile risk though; the unbelievable prices for Pakistani defence forces, and the huge selection, meant that I ended up buying much more than I needed. She did all the talking. We quietly paid our bills and left.

Chikan embroidery or chikankari is a traditional white-on-white hand embroidery, both delicate and beautiful, that gives it a lace-like look. It is the traditional summer-wear in Lucknow, the capital city of India's most populous state, Uttar Pradesh, and my mother's hometown. A Geographical Indication (GI) status was accorded for the 400-year-old art of chikankari in December 2008, recognizing Lucknow as an exclusive hub of chikankari. Being summer wear, it is done on light fabrics, traditionally muslin. In modern times, chiffon, crepe silk, organza and net fabrics are increasingly popular. These days, it is fashionably done on a variety of silk that can be worn in winters too. Coloured threads or fabrics are also popular. Its introduction in India is popularly credited to Noor Jahan, Mughal empress and wife of Emperor Jahangir. A version of chikankari is also done in Pakistan. The chikankari at the Naval Colony market was embellished with delicate Mukaish work, done by inserting and twisting fine metal wires into the fabric. I still have one of the cherished fabrics!

Visits to Lahore were always welcome. Lahore had a very vibrant intellectual and social life. People of Lahore were proud of their city and would always cite a Punjabi saying, '*Jinney Lahore nai vekhya, O jameya nai*,' meaning, 'One who hasn't seen Lahore, isn't even born,' or more simply, 'One has seen nothing, if one hasn't seen Lahore.' We enjoyed our first takatak at Laxmi Chowk in central Lahore. The chowk got its name from Lakshmi building, which was built way back in 1935. Lakshmi Chowk had some popular eateries and was renowned for its takatak, a dish made with assorted meat pieces on a large iron tawa, or flat griddle, with metal spoons making rhythmic sounds of *tak-a-tak*. This beautiful heritage of Lahore seems to have been lost now as Lakshmi Chowk was reportedly renamed Maulana Zafar Ali Chowk. Apparently, the facade of the heritage building got a coat of unwelcome paint that covers the gracefully aged building.

I was introduced to shopping in Lahore by my friend Safina. No trip to the city was ever complete without several trips to the market with Safina. She helped in choosing the fabrics and even introduced me to her jeweller. Later, when we were in India, she got some suits made for me and brought them with her on her trip to India with her husband, Raja, who did some business with India at the time.

The markets in Lahore were a woman's delight. With a guide like Safina, who knew her way around, it was an exciting adventure each time. Safina, Raja and their family were like a home away from home. They introduced us to different aspects of Lahore, including Lakshmi Chowk. Unfortunately, the friendship did not survive our nomadic lives; we lost touch with the family some years after leaving Islamabad.

Kaiser Monnoo, of the well-established Monnoo group, would address Ghanashyam as 'Sufi saab'. He treated us affectionately like young people from his own family. We had met him in Bonn at the residence of S.K. Lambah, the then India's ambassador to Germany. Kaiser Monnoo was quite a globetrotter. On one of his trips to Vietnam, he bought two identical paintings, got them framed in Lahore, hung one in his living room and gifted us the other one. Till today, that painting hangs proudly in our living room. The story of how it came to hang in our living room is one of Ghanashyam's favourites.

Lahore is home to many of Pakistan's liberal society. The home of Asma Jilani Jahangir, human rights lawyer and social activist, was a popular meeting point for Lahore's intellectuals. At times, we met some well-known Pakistani and Indian journalists at her home. She was a generous lady, with a ready smile but a steely spine.

On one occasion at her house, a Lahori friend surprised me by listing Indian Islamic heritage sites as belonging to Pakistan, starting with the Taj Mahal, saying, 'We lost this to you.' Thankfully, before I could give a stern response, he added, 'Now, only we are left. Since you have all this heritage, why don't you just take us as well!'

The home of Raza Kazim, a successful lawyer in Lahore, used to be a regular stopover for us every time we were in Lahore. He handled a few cases per year, earning enough for the whole year. He was passionate about Hindustani classical music and had even invented a musical instrument that his daughter would play. He had set up his own recording studio in the top floor of his sprawling bungalow where he recorded classical Hindustani music with very high fidelity. He would often organize classical music performances by Indian artists in Lahore and Islamabad. It was a blessing to have heard Pandit Jasraj sing in Islamabad, as it was to hear Pandit Shiv Prasad Chaurasia play the flute one night. It was delightful talking to Raza Kazim about classical Indian music.

We had enormous respect and admiration for his political life, which began as a child during the Quit India movement of 1942. It was common knowledge that he had been imprisoned by three Pakistani leaders. General Ayub Khan and Zulfikar Ali Bhutto had imprisoned him for refusing to become a cabinet minister, while General Muhammad Zia-ul-Haq accused him of attempting a coup d'état. He expressed his political views openly and fearlessly.

Raza Kazim's mother could not reconcile to leaving her home in India post Partition and never thought of Lahore or Pakistan as her home. She saw people from India as links to her long-lost land. Her longing for her place of birth touched me deeply.

Nostalgia for India was commonplace among women who came to Pakistan after marriage. With my family links to Lucknow, and having studied in Bhopal, I knew girls who had moved to Pakistan after marriage. I would often be reminded of them, when I saw women queuing up for Indian visas at our High Commission.

On one occasion, though, I was taken by surprise by one of them. I was waiting to enter the High Commission one morning and saw a young lady looking at me intently. She was talking to the security staff. Thinking of my friends from India who were in Pakistan, I gave her a smile. She promptly came over. I thought she needed some assistance. When she reached the car, she asked me, 'Are you a Hindu?' No one had ever asked me that question. 'I am Indian, but yes, I am a Hindu. Why do you ask?' I responded. Her response stunned me. 'I have never seen a Hindu,' she said. For a moment, I felt as if I was a caged animal in a zoo. I realized how fortunate we are in India to have such a rich diversity, with people of different faiths living side by side. We learn about culture and festivals of different faiths from our school days, often celebrating festivals together. 'Thankfully, India isn't a monochromatic society,' I thought to myself.

Indian-origin spouses of Pakistani defence personnel were perhaps most nostalgic of all. One of them was married to a celebrated retired Pakistan Army officer who had fought three wars against India. His family had migrated from India at the time of Partition. The wife had been the beloved first daughter of her father. She was born and raised in India, moving to Pakistan at the time of her marriage to a young Pakistan Army officer. Initially, life away from her family in India was smooth and happy. Her husband found it difficult to meet with her family due to restrictions on him as an army officer, but she was able to travel to India. Letters from her family kept her in touch with them. Then came the 1965 War with India, followed a few years later by the 1971 War. Though postal service was not banned, it was disrupted due to the prevailing situation of the time. 'Our letters would be transmitted via London during the war,' she once recalled sadly. 'I was even unable to see my dear father one last time before he passed on, nor could I attend his burial,' she recalled with moist eyes.

Her husband, the famous army officer, carried his own burden of nostalgia. Though he had led battles and wars against India, he too retained India in some corner of his heart. Once we were invited to a dinner at their house. It was an honour for young and relatively junior officers like us to be invited by a senior and well-known army officer, even a retired one. It was even more generous of him to show us around and share stories of the beautiful souvenirs in their house. At the end of the tour, Ghanashyam asked him, 'You have so many beautiful things from different parts of the world. How is it that you have nothing from India?' Referring to his origin in India, he responded humbly, '*Aur yeh nacheez kahan se hai?*' (Where do you think is this humble individual from?)

A. Milani, a human rights activist and columnist who ran an NGO for protection of children, was another good friend with whom we shared laughs and enjoyed many evenings together. He once took us home to meet his father, who was bedridden. He had got his father a contraption from the US that enabled him to tune into some radio frequencies and participate in family conversations. This had become one of his toys that enabled him to pass time.

Milani held a dinner for us when we were leaving Islamabad. There was a beautiful metal *jharokha* hanging in his living room.[1] We had been looking to buy one of those handicrafts but had not found a good one in Islamabad; the beautiful metal work was more readily available in Lahore. Ghanashyam asked him for guidance on where good handicrafts like that could be bought in Islamabad. He evaded the question, saying he could not remember where they got it from. When we were leaving after dinner, we found that the jharokha had been wrapped in paper and kept in our car! He overlooked all our protests. That jharokha has been our treasured possession and reminds us of the time spent with him and his family.

Khan Saheb was our landlord. A tall and handsome Pathan from the Federally Administered Tribal Areas (FATA)[2], he was

---

[1] Jharokha: An ornamental window, one of the most distinctive characteristics of the façade in medieval Indian architecture until the nineteenth century.
[2] Bordering Afghanistan

well connected and affluent. Khan Saheb was a deeply religious man, strongly connected with his Pathan roots. We became good friends with him and his family. His wife often accompanied him on his visits to Islamabad. They would stay in the one-bedroom apartment they had at the back of the house we lived in. On one occasion, Khan Saheb and his wife prepared a typical Peshawari dinner for us in their little apartment and invited us over. FATA was out of bounds for Indian diplomats, this was the next best invitation possible. His young son accompanied his parents on one occasion. As there was only one bedroom in his apartment, the son stayed with us at our home. Those were our only house guests in Islamabad!

Khan Saheb firmly believed that Peshawar had the best goat meat in Pakistan. He would invariably bring generous amounts of meat with him when he came. We would have it cooked and eat it together. He would always say, '*Bibi, hamare Pathanon mein kahte hain ki hafte mein kam se kam ek bar gosht kha liya karo. Imaan tazaa rahta hai!*' (Bibi, it is said among us Pathans that one should eat meat at least once a week. It refreshes one's faith!) He would leave his home in the morning, buy meat in Peshawar and drive straight to Islamabad.

Twice a year, before Eid and Diwali, the High Commission would get sweets from India for distribution among the Mission's friends and contacts. Indian sweets were popular in Pakistan, winning hands down over Pakistani ones. Kaju Katli, a delicacy made from cashews, was much in demand as cashews did not grow in Pakistan. The sweet burfi also has a longer shelf life. The High Commission's bus would go from Islamabad to Delhi with a couple of officials with lists from all the officers. They would get Kaju Katli from Delhi's most well-known sweet shop. The consolidated list used to fill the big bus with boxes of sweets. It would take several hours of loading at night in Delhi before the bus could start for Lahore. There, they would hand over the boxes for people in Lahore at the Indian Airlines' office before proceeding for Islamabad, from where we would further distribute sweets to our friends. Some boxes were sent to Karachi and Charsadda to the home town of the family of Frontier Gandhi, Khan Abdul Ghaffar Khan.

I was very fond of motichoor ke laddoo and would always get a couple of boxes of those for myself. Once Khan Saheb was visiting when the sweets arrived. We handed over his box of cashew burfi and offered him some warmed up motichoor ke laddoo. Khan Saheb was bemused by my fondness for the humble laddoo. I explained to him, 'This is different from the normal boondi laddoo, Khan Saheb. When it breaks, the little balls spread like pearls on your plate!' (*Moti ki tarah choor choor ho jaata hai*). I don't know whether it was the taste or my fanciful description, but Khan Saheb would always ask for motichoor ke laddoo after that day.

One person from Islamabad that I remember fondly is my tailor. Masterji was a slightly obese and burly man. He was always dressed in a Pathan suit favoured by Pakistani men. The loose salwar-kameez kept him comfortable and cool in the tiny space behind his counter that served as a place to interact with his customers as well as a cutting table. Masterji was from Bahawalpur. He would speak proudly of things made in his home town. 'The best dupattas are manufactured in Bahawalpur, Baji [elder sister]. Next time I go to Bahawalpur, I'll get you a full *thaan* [roll of fabric] from the factory,' he would always promise. True to his word, he did get me a roll of dupatta fabric, which I shared with family and friends.

Masterji always delayed my work. Once I complained: 'I give you all my work and yet you take so much time; long after others who gave you the fabric at the same time as I did!' He immediately took down a few of the ready pieces kept for delivery and showed me the difference in the finish between what he gave me and the things that were ready for others. He silenced me by saying, 'Baji, I personally supervise your work. It is never left to others.'

Masterji had a young son. A few days before our final departure from Islamabad, I went to pick up my last few suits from Masterji. The little boy was playing silently outside. 'He can neither hear, nor speak, Baji,' Masterji said with obvious sorrow and affection. We were packing our things in preparation for our final departure. Our children had quality bicycles that we had bought for them in Brussels. The younger son's bike seemed perfect for this silent little boy. So, I returned immediately with the bike and handed it over to him. To be fair to both my children, I gave the older son's mountain bike to our gardener. The shinning eyes of Masterji's little boy compensated me for the disappointment and anger of my children.

At shopping establishments, people in Pakistan would often treat us with greater courtesy than the locals. Sometimes shopkeepers would even offer me lunch or snacks like samosas or chaat, which on occasion elicited complaints from my Pakistani friends, '*Hamein to kabhi offer nahin kiya*!' (We never received this offer!) Even the doctors at the hospital seemed more courteous and attentive. This warmth and friendship compensated for the aggressive tailing by Pakistani agents.

I often wondered why Pakistanis were so courteous to us. A love–hate relationship normally refers to ups and downs in ties. This phrase seemed to have a double meaning for India and Pakistan: the vicissitudes in bilateral ties resembling a yo-yo, as also the contrasting warmth between the official relationship and that between the two peoples.

4

The Kahuta Adventure

'Why can't you ever get ready in time?' Ghanashyam was exasperated as usual at my tardiness. He wanted to be punctual. I did too, but invariably got distracted with home or children. It was also a struggle to tear myself away from spending time with the children after spending the day at work. He normally understood, but this was a special day for Ghanashyam; his dear friend Aftab was getting engaged.

Aftab was an economic analyst at one of the international banks in Islamabad. His family had migrated to Pakistan from southern India. It was their mutual love for economics that bound the two. Ghanashyam would avidly read Aftab's weekly economic analysis of Pakistan's economy. They would have long discussions on the subject. The bad days for Pakistan's economy had started even before we arrived in Islamabad, but the situation had become worse, with periodic threats of a Pakistani default on interest payments on its international loans.

Aftab would often bounce his ideas with Ghanashyam. He would periodically seek inputs on India's liberalization process and the lessons it held for management of Pakistan's economy. Ghanashyam once asked him, 'How do you manage the intelligence people? Don't they harass you for meeting me frequently?' Aftab managed the agencies by telling them that he was brainstorming on India's economic management to recommend solutions to the Government of Pakistan. He had told them, 'If you want, I'll stop seeing him. But then you'll have to tell the Pakistan government why I can't give them ideas on the economy.' That was enough to stop the questioning, he said.

We reached Aftab's house a bit late for his engagement party. As usual, the agents followed us in their white Toyota Corolla and went off for dinner once we were inside.

Aftab's home seemed somewhat desolate. There were a few people, but no family, or decorations. We sat with his friends on the terrace. 'Perhaps we are a bit early,' I thought to myself. But as time passed, I started wondering what was happening.

The mystery cleared around 9 p.m. when the agents following us, normally went off duty. Aftab suddenly appeared on the terrace and disclosed that the party was at a farmhouse on the outskirts of Islamabad. The few people present started moving out to take their cars to proceed to the farmhouse. Aftab asked that we wait in the house with his friend and leave with him after five to ten minutes, so that he could receive us at the venue. He also suggested that we travel in his friend's car. We were perplexed. We had a small Mitsubishi Pajero SUV that we had bought from a departing Japanese diplomat recently. It was in excellent condition, with hardly any mileage. They evasively responded that a Pajero was unsuitable for the journey. I was still confused. 'An SUV would surely be better placed to navigate bad roads, if that's the problem,' I commented. 'The road is fairly narrow in places,' he responded. Finally, we started in his friend's car for the farmhouse ten minutes after Aftab's departure. We sat in the back seat; the friend sat in the front, with the driver.

Soon after leaving Islamabad, the road entered a green and forested area. Aftab's friend was a friendly person who kept up a cheerful conversation going, narrating stories of Pakistani life. We were happily laughing together, when he announced, 'We will soon pass the Radar Station located off the road to our left. It is well guarded by soldiers. But actually, the radars here don't work; only the radars on the hill are working!'

The happy smile on my face suddenly vanished. I realized that we were outside the permitted area without permission to travel to the destination we were headed to. 'I could not even pass off for a local with my traditional Indian silk sari,' I thought. Suddenly, I remembered the big bindi I was wearing, which revealed my Indian and Hindu identity. The modern-day avatar of the bindi is a 'stick-on' version. I quietly removed it from my forehead and hid it behind the sari at the nape of my neck. 'Ghanashyam with his beard would probably pass off for a Pakistani and I could pretend to be a Mohajir,' I tried to reassure myself.[1]

Almost as soon as I had transferred my bindi to its hiding place, we passed Pakistani soldiers beside the road, guarding the entrance to what we had just learnt was Pakistan's defunct radar station! It was on my side of the road. The soldiers were just a few feet away from my window as the car passed them by. Thankfully, they did not stop the innocuous looking Toyota Corolla with a local number plate. 'Good thing we are not in our bright green and orange Pajero, with an Indian diplomatic number plate,' I thought, as I heaved a sigh of relief.

---

[1] The Pakistanis who migrated from India after Partition are still called Mohajirs, based on the Arabic word for migrants. Technically, Mohammed Ali Jinnah, the founder of Pakistan, was also one of them. Many Mohajir women prefer wearing saris.

The adventure was far from over, though. A few minutes later, pointing to the right side of the road, Aftab's friend said that very soon we would be driving past the missile development facilities of Pakistan. This raised my anxiety levels even further.

We drove another few minutes before reaching our destination: a luxurious farmhouse near Kahuta, the home of Pakistan's nuclear facilities at Khan Research Laboratories. It is Pakistan's main facility for the development of nuclear weapons. No guesses were needed to know that this was a complete 'no-go' area for Indians. We were, however, in a local's car, completely unaware of the destination, with no way to go back to Islamabad.

The thought raced through my mind that the airspace over Kahuta was not available for over flights; as it struck me that Kahuta was probably included in the list of Pakistan's prohibited airspaces, where overflights were not allowed; an aircraft violating a prohibited airspace would be intercepted and face the possibility of an attack. It would be safe to presume that we would have been the only Indian diplomats to have ever ventured to this area.

We entered the sprawling lawns of the farmhouse, apprehensive but with brave, beaming smiles on our faces. Once inside the party area, our smiles were replaced with a look of incredulity. The party was spread over an enormous area. The who's who of Pakistani society seemed to be present, including former foreign secretaries, former ambassadors to India, and erstwhile seniors from defence and security fields. Those we met were too polite to ask us what we were doing in that prohibited zone, but their quizzical looks seemed to ask the question.

Apart from the discomfort of knowing that we were in the wrong place, it was a grand party. The atmosphere was relaxed, and people mingled without inhibitions. The legendary Pakistani hospitality was on full display, with delicious and plentiful food all around. There was no doubt that the crème de la crème of Islamabad society had gathered that evening for the party.

I was jolted by the sound of some familiar music. The party seemed to suddenly liven up to the sound of '*Jai Jai Shiv Shankar*' on the public address system. The peppy and popular Bollywood number wasn't the only Indian song played that evening. No one saw the irony of the musical sounds from India taking over the air of Kahuta's neighbourhood, as several of the guests were uninhibited in their enjoyment of the Bollywood magic on the dance floor.

We returned to Islamabad well past midnight. The return journey was uneventful. We went with Aftab's friend to our car parked at his house and drove home innocently. I wondered what happened to the intelligence agents following us that night. We were seen by hundreds of people that evening in a prohibited area, that too in an area subjected to the highest security protection in Pakistan.

The Engineering Research Laboratories (ERL), Pakistan's key uranium enrichment facility, is located in Kahuta. Renamed Khan Research Laboratories (KRL) in May 1981, it uses centrifuges to produce highly enriched uranium.

Pakistan's nuclear ambitions were set in earnest by Zulfikar Ali Bhutto in 1975, soon after India's peaceful nuclear explosion of 1974. Its nuclear dream really took off once physicist Dr Abdul Qadeer Khan returned to Pakistan with stolen centrifuge designs from the Physical Dynamic Research Laboratory (FDO) in the Netherlands.[2] A report in the *Guardian* newspaper some years

---

[2] William J. Broad and David E. Sanger, 'A Tale of Nuclear Proliferation: How Pakistani Built His Network', *New York Times*, 12 February 2004.

From his perch at Urenco, a European consortium, he possessed blueprints of the world's best centrifuges—the hollow metal tubes that spin very fast to enrich natural uranium into bomb fuel.
A set of thousands of centrifuges, called a cascade, concentrates the rare U-235 isotope to make a potent fuel.

later also recalled that after he left Holland, A.Q. Khan was sentenced to four years in prison by an Amsterdam court for industrial espionage—allegedly for stealing sensitive enrichment technology blueprints. The sentence was later dismissed on appeal.[3]

A metallurgical engineer and nuclear weapon technologist, trained in Germany and the Netherlands, with a PhD in metallurgical engineering from Belgium, Khan began working in May 1972 at the FDO, a subcontractor of Ultra Centrifuge Nederland (UCN), the Dutch partner in the Urenco uranium enrichment consortium. He had spent years at the FDO and accessed the most confidential sites and information. In December 1975, he is alleged to have suddenly left the FDO for Pakistan with copies of blueprints for centrifuges and other components. He also carried with him information of nearly 100 companies supplying centrifuge components and materials. He established an elaborate procurement network that obtained nuclear technology for KRL.

A.Q. Khan first started centrifuge work at the Pakistan Atomic Energy Commission (PAEC), which was headed by Munir Ahmad Khan. However, conflicts soon emerged, and Khan received autonomous control over Pakistan's uranium enrichment programmes, setting up ERL on 31 July 1976.

'I saw top-secret technical drawings in his house,' recalled Frits Veerman, a Dutch colleague who shared an office with Dr. Khan.
Dr. Khan stole the designs, Dutch investigators found, and he fled back to Pakistan in 1976. He used the blueprints and his knowledge to set up an enrichment project in Kahuta, near Islamabad, that reported directly to the prime minister. He drew heavily on Dutch lists of nearly 100 companies that supplied centrifuge parts and materials.

[3] Owen Bowcott, 'Abdul Qadeer Khan: Pakistani nuclear scientist accused of industrial espionage', *Guardian*, 6 February 2009.

Though better known for its work on the nuclear programme, the Kahuta facility was also involved in Pakistan's missile development programme, at a ballistic missile research centre at Kahuta. Intermediate-Range Ballistic Missiles based on liquid fuel technology were said to have been developed and tested there. KRL carried out a test flight of the medium-range Ghauri–I/Hatf-5 missile on 6 April 1998, identified by US intelligence officials as the North Korean Nodong missile.[4] Pakistani media had also carried a reference to the visit of Saudi Prince Sultan bin Abdul Aziz to the Kahuta facility in May 1999, possibly in connection with purchases of the Ghauri missiles.

There was strong interest among foreign intelligence agencies, including the US and erstwhile Soviet Union, in Pakistan's nuclear programme. There is an interesting, though unverified account of how India confirmed the existence of the nuclear facility at Kahuta. Apparently, the Research and Analysis Wing (R&AW), India's intelligence agency, picked up 'chatter' about the possible existence of a fissile material production facility. Pakistan kept this facility so much under wraps that no specific information or the location of the facility or confirmation of the rumours had been possible. Indian agents managed to obtain the fallen hair samples from the barber shops in Kahuta where the nuclear scientists came to get their hair cut. An analysis of these samples for radiation traces revealed that the Kahuta plant was a plutonium refining plant to develop an atomic bomb.[5] Another unconfirmed report in the media claimed that former prime minister Morarji Desai, in a telephonic conversation with the then martial law administrator, Zia-ul-Haq, let it slip, that the Indian government knew about

---

[4] Nuclear Threat Initiative, NTI.org.
[5] Raghav Gakhar, 'Operation Kahuta: When RAW Agents Almost Reached the Pakistan Nuclear Reactor', DefenceLover, 23 July 2017; also carried by defence update.

Pakistan's secret nuclear bomb-making facility at Kahuta, thereby exposing the Indian agency's network in Pakistan. Thus alerted, Zia proceeded to destroy the R&AW network in Pakistan.[6]

Once the facility at Kahuta was established, there were concerns about protecting it from foreign attack. This became a priority as it was realized that Kahuta was just a few minutes (around three minutes) from the Line of Control as the crow flies and that the Indian Air Force could attack the facility and safely return before the Pakistan Air Force could get to the site. It is said that this realization prompted Pakistan's effort to upgrade its air defences by, among other measures, the acquisition of F-16 fighting jets to acquire the capability to mount a retaliatory attack on India's nuclear research facilities in Trombay.

India was not the only country interested in the Kahuta facilities. A senior Pakistani military official claimed to have successfully thwarted a CIA plot to target nuclear scientists and engineers associated with Pakistan's nuclear programme in 1979 and some undercover CIA agents and US diplomats were declared personae non grata around this time.[7]

Following our visit to the farmhouse in Kahuta, one heard the story of the arrest of the French ambassador to Pakistan, Pol Le Gourrierec, and his first secretary, Jean Forlot, in the vicinity of the KRL nuclear complex on 26 June 1979. Apparently, they were travelling in a car without a flag or a diplomatic number plate. The ambassador and the first secretary were both injured in the altercation that followed. Their cameras and other sensitive equipment were confiscated. There were claims by Pakistan that they were spying for the CIA, while the diplomats claimed

---

[6] Uday Mahurkar, 'How Morarji Desai helped Pakistan become a nuclear state', dailyO, 24 June 2015.

[7] Ansar Abbasi, 'Brig Imtiaz reveals CIA plots', News, 1 September 2009.

that they had taken a wrong turn and were accidentally in the proximity of the nuclear facility.

An account in Pakistan's *Dawn* newspaper[8] alleged Indo-Israeli collaboration for eliminating Pakistan's nuclear capability based on the book *Deception: Pakistan, the United States and the Global Nuclear Weapons Conspiracy* by investigative journalists Adrian Levy and Catherine Scott-Clark. It claimed that the plan was for bombing Kahuta by Israeli planes using Indian bases.[9] The plans were said to be abandoned due to US pressure and Pakistan's threat to retaliate against the Bhabha Atomic Research Centre (BARC) in Trombay. The report claimed that the plans were called off after increased air defence around the Kahuta plant robbed the element of surprise, which was the chief component of the alleged plan. The US Department of State's declassified top-secret documents from 1984 to 1985 showed that the US ambassador in Islamabad had in his talking points issued a warning about an Indian military attack on the Kahuta nuclear plant.[10] Declassified documents in the Hungarian archives also showed that the Soviets had shared with the Hungarians India's plans to attack Kahuta.[11] It is said that periodic rumours and unfounded stories in the Western media about India's covert plans to attack Kahuta, led India to discuss the Agreement on the Prohibition of Attack against Nuclear

---

[8] Shaikh Aziz, 'A Leaf from History: Defending Kahuta', *Dawn*, 26 July 2015.

[9] Israel, it was claimed, wanted to use Gujarat's Jamnagar base to launch its jets, refuel at a satellite airfield in north India and track the Himalayas to avoid early radar detection.

[10] Sushant Sareen, 'In fact: Did India plan a covert military attack on a Pakistani nuclear reactor?' *Indian Express*, 26 October 2015.

[11] Ibid.; Based on Sergey Radchenko and Artemy M. Kalinovsky, *The End of the Cold War and the Third World: New Perspectives on Regional Conflict*, Routledge, 2013.

Installations and Facilities between India and Pakistan, which was eventually signed in 1988.

The presence of Indian diplomats anywhere in or around Kahuta would raise alarm bells in the Pakistani intelligence agencies. Any slip could have had serious consequences not just for us individually, but also on bilateral relations between India and Pakistan. At the very least, we would have been declared personae non grata, but at worse, it could have meant a prolonged stay languishing in Pakistani custody. Aftab probably understood this. He may have had links in the right places and got an informal clearance for our participation in his engagement party. Perhaps he realized that we would simply have refused to attend the party if we knew that the location of the venue was in Kahuta. He must have been confident of handling the objections of the authorities to the presence of Indian diplomats in the vicinity of Pakistan's most secure facilities. Aftab's reasons for the deception including hiding the details from us, have remained a mystery!

5

Love across the Border

The partition of India did not just draw a line on a map dividing Mother India between its warring children—the Muslims going to East and West Pakistan, while the majority consisting of Hindus, Sikhs, Christians, Buddhists and Jains remaining in India. Partition drew a line across the hearts of people, dividing families and loved ones, snatching properties, and turning affluent and well-to-do people to destitution.

At the time of India's independence, British India was divided into India and Pakistan. The latter comprised West and East Pakistan; East Pakistan later became Bangladesh. Partition is an extremely violent and difficult chapter in India's history. Almost 10–20 million people were displaced on religious lines; Muslims from India moved to Pakistan, while Hindus and Sikhs migrated from various parts of Pakistan to India. An estimated two-thirds of the Muslims lived in East and West Pakistan at the time of Partition, but about one-third of the Muslims lived in India. Following Partition, massive exchanges of population took place, accompanied by unimaginable violence. Based on the 1951 census of displaced persons, around 72,26,000 Muslims went to Pakistan from India, while 72,49,000 Hindus and Sikhs moved to India from Pakistan.[1] The number of people killed due to the violence at the time of Partition is estimated to range between 2,00,000 to as high as 2 million. These events cast a long shadow on the relationship between India and Pakistan.

Around 200 million Muslims[2] are estimated to live in India, which has the world's third-highest Muslim population. Several of the Muslims who stayed back were not convinced about the partition of India on religious lines. They believed instead in the concept of a secular nation. Others stayed for more practical reasons such as property owned, attachment to one's place of birth or simply the lack of means to migrate. Among many Muslim families, one brother stayed back in India, while the other migrated to Pakistan. West Punjab (in Pakistan) was effectively 'cleansed' of its minority population. There are hardly any Hindus and Sikhs there; they are mostly to be found in the provinces of Sindh, Balochistan and North-West Frontier Province (NWFP).

The pain of separation was acutely felt by the divided Muslim families. They feared that a generation or two later, their progenies may not even know each other. Many families tried to continue the family links across the border into the next generation through marriage. Several Muslim families have a daughter or a son living across the border in the other country, keeping the memories of the undivided family alive.

---

[1] Vivek Shukla, 'When Muslims left Pakistan for India', *New Indian Express*, 14 August 2017.

[2] India's Muslims numbered 172.2 million, being 14.2 per cent of India's population, according to the 2011 census, thus, making Islam India's second-largest religion.

In Islamabad, we were once surprised by a total stranger. He had identified us as Indians from the number plate of our car. He came to us out of the blue in the crowded Aabpara market to tell us that his brother lived in India. 'I just cannot fight a war with India,' he said. 'How would I know that the bomb I drop across the border is not going to fall on my brother's house?' Yet, India and Pakistan have fought four wars, including one limited war (in Kargil), and the Pakistan Army had by then been led by two army chiefs whose families had migrated from India.

India's partition also drew a line of distrust among communities. After Partition, it took decades for the minority and majority community in India to find an uneasy modus vivendi. Interfaith marriages between the two communities were (and still are) rare and frowned upon. Marriages across the border, unless for family reasons, were unheard of. A marriage between two people belonging to different faiths with their families on two sides of the border was a rare phenomenon. The religious fault lines seem to have deepened over the years.

None of this occurred to Vikas and Zeenat when they fell in love.

Zeenat came from a divided Mohajir family. Her father's family had been well settled in Lucknow; her uncle still lived there. Lucknow, the capital of the north Indian state of Uttar Pradesh, is home to many a Mohajir family in Pakistan. Her mother, Nusrat's, family had also moved to Pakistan from India. Zeenat's father, Majid, was a successful energy consultant and her mother, Nusrat, a successful banker. They lived not far from where we did.

I no longer remember how we became friends, or how we met even. Nusrat remembers that we met at a national day reception in Islamabad. It was the beautiful sari in shades of blue and my cropped hair that worked for her. Nusrat always dressed in lovely saris herself and with her short hair, uncommon in Pakistan, she stood out as a smart, confident and warm person. She was won over by my 'enthusiastic voice, full of conviction', while I responded to the same qualities in her. Perhaps, I most appreciated her honesty and commitment to liberal causes. She was aghast that her friends in Karachi, who were liberals like her until recently, had taken to the hijab and become ultra conservative. Pakistan's rapid turn to religious orthodoxy worried her. She once pointed with concern to the growing numbers of cars outside mosques in Islamabad for namaz (Friday prayers). We put aside the concern and decided that it was a good time to meet for lunch as those shadowing me also went to the mosque for the Friday congregations!

We were once sitting in the garden of a retired lieutenant general of the Pakistan Army with a small group of women. Most of the others in the group were linked to the Pakistan defence forces through their spouses. They were talking about the difficult visa regime prevailing between the two countries, when Nusrat spoke clearly, 'It would make a lot of sense for Pakistan to have an open border with India. Pakistani visitors to India would benefit from India's liberal society and from seeing the economic progress that India is making. But from India's perspective, it would make sense to raise the hardest curtain and stop all influences coming from Pakistan. We can only send extremist and fundamentalist conservative ideology from Pakistan!' Her articulation was so honest and confident that no one in the group challenged her.

Nusrat and I developed a close friendship that has survived the years and the distance separating us. My boys loved spending time at her home with her daughters. That was the only house of 'girls' that they would deign to visit. We tried to meet outside the duty hours of the Pakistani intelligence shadowing us, sometimes visiting each other after 9 p.m. when the agents went off duty. It helped that Ghanashyam and Majid shared an interest in oil and energy. They too became good friends.

Zeenat was the eldest. Beautiful and bright, she was a warm, sensitive and dignified teenager in those days. With her brilliant academic performance, it was no surprise that she was studying for her master's at the London School of Economics. Given her pretty looks, bright mind and good family, there was no dearth of appropriate proposals.

'When can we meet for lunch, Ruchi?' Nusrat called me one day. She seemed somewhat preoccupied, so we fixed an appointment for lunch the very next day. We met as arranged at a small, somewhat informal restaurant. As usual, we started chatting about Pakistani politics and economy, before diverting to other general issues.

'Zeenat is in love with an Indian boy she met in London,' Nusrat suddenly blurted out. 'And he's not even Muslim! She's fallen for a Punjabi-Hindu boy,' she added.

I could understand her anxiety. Of all the people in India, the Punjabi Hindus are thought to be the most bitter about Partition. Being a border state, it was divided into two at the time of Partition—the Hindu-majority areas became a part of India, while the Muslim-majority areas went to Pakistan. The people of the state witnessed the worst horrors of Partition caused by one of the world's most brutal mass migrations. A good number of Punjabis in India had a deep mistrust of not just Pakistanis, but even Muslims as a community.

I felt that Nusrat was worried that the boy's family in India would never accept the relationship but soon discovered that her anxiety had many more dimensions. 'What do we know of the family?' said a worried Nusrat. 'We don't know what kind of people they are; or whether they even have a background that could keep up to the standards Zeenat has been brought up with,' she added. 'If she marries this boy, she would be living all alone in another country, one that may not really welcome her! Perhaps she would not even be welcomed by the boy's family!' Nusrat was clearly worried. They had never met the boy or his family. It was not the easiest thing to travel across the border from one country to the other. It was not just the physical distance but the deep gulf between the two peoples and communities that seemed like 'a bridge too far'.

Doubt and distrust were not just an Indian prerogative, I realized. Nusrat and Majid were aware of the trauma of Partition. Nusrat loved her daughter too much to doubt her choice, but Majid's love for his daughter translated to deep anxiety about Zeenat's prospects of happiness in India, especially in a Punjabi-Hindu family. He was convinced that the relationship should be terminated. While Nusrat shared her husband's concerns, she was sure of Zeenat's commitment to Vikas. She felt that it would not only be futile but disastrous to try and break up the relationship. She seemed convinced that efforts to separate Vikas and Zeenat could result in damaging their own relationship as parents with their daughter.

She was at her wit's end and torn between her love for Zeenat and her fears for her daughter. In some desperation, she asked if I would visit Vikas's family in Delhi to assess what they were dealing with. I periodically went to Delhi on 'Courier Duty' and agreed to try and get an early assignment, during which I could meet with Vikas and his family.

During my next visit to Delhi, I fixed up a meeting with Vikas's father in his office. He was running a successful chartered accountancy firm, with several employees and a large office in the heart of Delhi. He seemed like a friendly and jovial person. Vikas too seemed like a cultured, smart and well-educated person, a qualified chartered accountant, working in his father's office. They invited me to their home in the evening.

That evening, I realized how difficult it was going to be for the young couple. Vikas's parents mirrored Nusrat and Majid's views. They, too, felt that the match between Zeenat and Vikas would be a disaster. While Nusrat and Majid were worried about sending their daughter across the border, Vikas's parents were worried about how a Pakistani Muslim girl would be received by the conservative Delhi society. They also worried about the distance that such a relationship might create between their beloved son and his family. 'And what about the children?' they asked. Will they be brought up as Hindus or Muslims? Will they prefer India or Pakistan? These and a whole set of questions occupied their minds.

Soon after returning to Islamabad, Nusrat and I met to exchange notes. It was like a debriefing session. Nusrat was full of questions. She wanted to be reassured that her daughter wasn't about to make the biggest mistake of her life. She was relieved by my description of Vikas, his family, their successful office and their lovely home in one of the best-known localities of south Delhi. It was apparent that Zeenat would be very comfortable and that she would live in the style that she was used to at her parents' home. Vikas seemed as committed to her as she was to him, and that he would look after her through thick and thin. I had come away with a warm feeling after meeting Vikas and his family; they seemed like a nice and affectionate family, affluent and respected in society.

Thus convinced, Nusrat joined Zeenat's efforts to convince Majid, who remained unconvinced for a very long time. Vikas, too, diligently continued to discuss the future with his parents, while Ghanashyam and I remained a bridge that either side could use.

It took some time before both families were convinced. Vikas visited Pakistan and managed to soften Majid after several meals and games of golf. Finally, it was really Zeenat's transparent happiness when Vikas was around that eventually convinced Majid. Nusrat and Majid visited Delhi and met the family. We were, by this time, back in Delhi from Islamabad. After a long process of getting to know each other, the doubts on both sides melted away.

Zeenat and Vikas initially faced some teething troubles after the marriage. Zeenat's long-term visa to stay in India was an issue. But things soon settled down. They took an apartment in central Delhi, close to Vikas's office and then moved into Vikas's big family home. Today, they have two beautiful teenage children. Vikas has expanded the family business and transformed the scale of their operations. I have never asked if the children are being brought up as Hindus or Muslims, as the focus seems more on making them good human beings. Zeenat has found an interest in Hindu philosophy. During the Covid-19 pandemic, she maintained her calm and sanity by attending an online course on the Bhagavad Gita that she recommended to me.

Some years after marriage, Nusrat and Majid migrated to Canada as their other two daughters, younger sisters of Zeenat, had settled in the US after marriage. With her parents moving out of Pakistan, Zeenat could visit them without worrying too much about visas. For Majid and Nusrat too, it became easier to travel to India. From Pakistan, they once had to take a flight to India via Dubai, with an eight-hour halt at the airport in Dubai.

These days, when I see Vikas and Zeenat's happiness together, it gladdens my heart that we could play a small role in a young couple's quest to achieve their destiny together. It would have been a pity if politics had succeeded in keeping them apart.

6

The Politician's Wife

Those days, there was quite a demand in India for Pakistani goods. Handicrafts made from Pakistani onyx stone were highly sought after. Women friends in India would often ask about designer Pakistani outfits and dress materials. Pakistani cotton prints and machine-made chikan embroidery on cotton fabric were preferred in the north Indian summer. Indian women were even familiar with the pricey Pakistani designer chikan fabric brand 'Bareeze'. I would often be asked about 'Bareeze' fabric, especially 'Bareeze' on Swiss cotton!

Pakistani women had their own fashion trends. They wore the salwars a little above the ankles. The elegant silver anklets on bare ankles did not seem to offend the conservative Islamic dress code. Their kurtas were cut differently. Pakistani women preferred a straight, slim and tailored look, with a long slit on the sides. Kurtas in Western designs in plain fabrics, with velvet trimmings, plain silk suits with printed or checked dupattas or stoles were another fashion trend. In India, women those days had started wearing ready-made salwar suits, often ill-fitted, with an A-line cut. Travelling to India from Pakistan, I often felt that Indian women sometimes resembled a sack of potatoes, compared to their elegant-looking Pakistani counterparts in their fashionable straight cuts and well-fitted clothes. The ready-made garments industry has since smartened up in India; these days, many brands selling smart and elegant ready-made ladies' clothes compete to catch the attention of Indian women.

It is a cliché that the grass is greener on the other side. Pakistani women saw my Indian silk saris and swooned with envy. Chinese silk fabrics sold by the yard were readily available in the markets of Islamabad, but Indian silk was not. Indian brocade and Banarasi silk suits were much in demand. Once at the Lahore airport, an unknown Pakistani official approached us when my husband and I were travelling to India. He requested that we bring a 'Banarasi Joda'[1] on return. His daughter was getting married and he wanted it for her wedding dress. I wondered how we would find him when we returned since we didn't even know his name! He said that he would keep an eye out for us as he was posted at the airport. We gave him the date of our return before leaving. While in Delhi, we bought a red silk Banarasi Joda at a state handloom store of the Uttar Pradesh government. The man at the airport was overjoyed to receive the gift for his daughter's wedding. We never asked his name or which part of the airport bureaucracy he worked for.

It wasn't just Indian Banarasi silk that was sought after in Pakistan. I was once asked to bring items from India to sell at the Indian women's stall at a charity bazar organized by Pakistan Foreign Office wives. I bought a suitcase full of 'designer' printed mill-made synthetic fabric saris from a small shop in one of

---

[1] Silk salwar kameez and stole in traditional festive Banarasi silk fabric. Banarasi silk saris are the preferred wedding saris due to their elaborate gold 'zari' work.

Delhi's popular markets, known for reasonable prices. I chose the brands advertised on TV channels with a viewership in Pakistan. Everything, including the handicrafts, sold like hot cakes in less than an hour despite our shamelessly high mark-up. The Indian women's stall was able to make a big contribution to charity.

Among the rich and well-off Pakistanis, Indian wedding jewellery was very popular. In fact, a lot of people came to India, both Delhi and Mumbai, for trousseau shopping. This business shifted to Dubai after the Indian visa regime became stricter for Pakistanis.

Like most of my Pakistani friends in Islamabad, I met Fatima at one of the receptions in Islamabad. She was married to a senior politician from Punjab, belonging to one of the two leading political parties of Pakistan. At the time of our meeting, her husband was well established in Lahore.

I liked Fatima immediately. She was a tall and handsome woman, confident of herself, and a warm and friendly person. She too seemed to enjoy talking to me. I hadn't met her before; being from Lahore, she was not often at the receptions in Islamabad. Fatima had visited India several times and enjoyed shopping in India.

A year or so after I had met her, Fatima spoke to me about a problem that she faced. She had bought jewellery for her daughter's engagement in Delhi. Her daughter loved most of what she had bought, but there were a few pieces that she needed to return. As she had not paid the full amount, returning the pieces would be a simple exercise and would not involve any financial transaction. She asked if I could find someone who could return the pieces to the jeweller in Delhi. I took the jeweller's telephone number and requested my father in Delhi to find out if the return of Fatima's jewellery pieces could be done easily. Once he had spoken to the people in Delhi, I told Fatima that I would help her out during my next visit to Delhi.

During my next 'courier duty', I fixed a meeting with Fatima at her home in Lahore during my transit there. There was no direct flight between Islamabad and Delhi and the journey involved several hours of transit at Lahore. As there was enough time, Fatima offered me some tea. We talked for some time and she gave me the jewellery to be returned in a small brocade pouch.

My father was kind enough to drive me to return the jewellery in Delhi. It wasn't a store, but someone's home in the Bengali Market area in central Delhi. We returned the jewellery with ease. The family seemed relieved to get the items back. They had given the pieces to Fatima on trust as she had run out of money at the time of shopping. She had promised to send the money after reaching Lahore. Once back, Fatima's daughter didn't like some of the items and instead of paying the balance, Fatima wanted to simply return some of the pieces. The return could not be done immediately, and the sellers in Delhi had started to get a little anxious. I informed Fatima of the return; the sellers in Delhi also called her to confirm the receipt of the items.

Fatima had been teaching at a college in Lahore during the military rule of General Zia-ul-Haq. During one of our meetings, she reminisced about the time in Pakistan when increasing restrictions under General Zia imposed limits on what they could or could not say during lectures in class. The constraints only got worse as Zia consolidated his hold over Pakistan. She described how a large number of people became political activists following the hanging of Zulfikar Ali Bhutto by General Zia. They eventually took to the streets protesting for restoring democracy in Pakistan. During this struggle, many of them were detained and arrested.

I was struck by the spirit of their struggle. Even though she herself had no direct involvement in politics, she was among those who took to the streets. As she spoke of her own struggle for democracy in Pakistan, I silently wondered how many of the intellectuals in India, belonging to my generation, had had to participate in street protests or been jailed for standing up against an unjust law or administration. I felt fortunate to have been born in India, as our post-Independence political journey seemed to have been easier than that of the Pakistani citizens. In India, we did not have to live under periodic impositions of martial law or military rule.

Several weeks after my visit to Lahore, I had a surprise call from Fatima. She was in Islamabad at her sister's house, not far from where we lived. She invited me to tea with them that evening as she was leaving the next day.

Fatima and her sister received me warmly later that evening. We sat and talked about life in Pakistan. It amused us to discuss the mutual fascination that we seemed to have for each other, despite the official political distance. Perhaps, it was the distance that caused people on each side to be curious about the other— the greater the distance, the more the curiosity.

During the easy-going conversation, I asked Fatima about Benazir Bhutto, Pakistan's first and only woman prime minister. I asked her about the stories one heard about corruption by Benazir's husband, Asif Ali Zardari, who was sometimes referred to as Mr 10 per cent in Pakistan[2] in those days, an allegation denied by the Pakistan People's Party (PPP). I was expecting her to hedge the question, or answer in an evasive manner. I was surprised when she responded in a matter-of-fact way.

She based her defence of Benazir Bhutto, the leader of the PPP, primarily on the challenges Benazir faced as the first woman prime

---

[2] 'Villain to some, hero to others: Asif Ali Zardari returns as Pakistan president', *Guardian*, 1 April 2024: Sharjeel Inam Memon, a senior Sindh minister, described the allegations against Zardari and the PPP as 'political propaganda and lies'. He said: 'We don't take any percentage on any project and no department is involved in taking any percentage. It is all baseless allegations.' John Bingham, 'Asif Ali Zardari: Life and Style of Pakistan's Mr 10 Per Cent', *Telegraph*, 3 August 2010.

minister of Pakistan. Benazir entered politics at a young age. At thirty-five, she became the world's youngest prime minister. She also became the first and youngest female prime minister ever elected in the Islamic world in modern history.

As the first woman to lead a democratic government in a Muslim country, challenges were to be expected, but these were compounded by the attitude of the right-wing military establishment of Pakistan. Benazir had struggled against military dictatorship as part of the Movement for the Restoration of Democracy, a political alliance formed in 1981 by the political parties opposing the military government of General Zia-ul-Haq. The Pakistani establishment felt threatened by her and saw her as an outlier. The Islamic fundamentalists opposed her, as they believed that it was un-Islamic for the country to have a female leader. They used her Western education and lifestyle abroad to project her as un-Islamic. The ISI even funded the creation of the Islami Jamhoori Ittehad (IJI)[3] and resorted to vote rigging to secure an IJI victory to prevent her from becoming the prime minister, she said.[4] In the elections that followed Zia's death, the PPP emerged with the largest block of seats, but without a clear majority. Benazir managed to become prime minister, but her opponents did not give up, Fatima explained.

In 1989, the Internal Wing of the ISI covertly tried to bring a vote of no confidence in Parliament to remove Benazir and trigger nationwide elections. This was allegedly done at the behest of the army chief and was prompted by differences over Afghanistan policy. The scandal was exposed by an intelligence agency that

---

[3] Nasir Iqbal, 'IJI funding case statements missing', *Dawn*, 1 March 2012.
[4] 'Ex-prime minister claims a "moral victory" but says "the election was stolen from us" through massive fraud.' Bob Drogin, 'Bhutto Loses Her Bid to Regain Power in Pakistan Vote', *Los Angeles Times*, 25 October 1990.

videotaped the attempt to financially influence and convince two senior members of Parliament belonging to the ruling party. The scandal came to be known as Operation Midnight Jackal.[5] Though the no-confidence motion against Benazir was defeated, President Ghulam Ishaq Khan dismissed Benazir's government under the Eighth Amendment of the Constitution in August 1990 attributing it to her government's corruption and inability to maintain law and order; a caretaker government led by former PPP member Ghulam Mustafa Jatoi was sworn in.

Fatima also gave a detailed account of the Mehrangate Scandal. She explained that during the Pakistan elections held in 1990, the ISI conspired against Benazir's campaign and that of her party, by systematically distributing campaign funding of taxpayers' money to several politicians to damage her campaign. Younis Habib, one of the main protagonists of the scandal and the former chief of the Mehran Bank, informed a court several years later that he had arranged for Pak Rs 1.48 billion, out of which Pak Rs 140 million was distributed among political parties,[6] while the rest were invested in army welfare schemes and transferred to account numbers provided by the ISI officials. He also revealed that Pak Rs 150 million was provided for the establishment of the Mehran Bank, which is why all the embezzlements were called the 'Mehrangate Scandal', although the money was drawn from Habib Bank Limited. Former ISI Chief General Asad Durrani revealed that the money was distributed to politicians on the directives of the then Army Chief General Mirza Aslam Baig (Retd) with the backing of the then President Ghulam Ishaq Khan.[7] A petition

---

[5] Shaikh Aziz, 'A leaf From History: When the "Midnight Jackals" didn't howl', *Dawn*, 27 November 2018.

[6] Nasir Iqbal 'Money arranged at behest of Ghulam Ishaq, Aslam Beg: Habib', *Dawn*, 9 March 2012.

[7] Jon Boone, 'Former ISI chief says army money used to influence 1990 Pakistan election', *Guardian*, 9 March 2012; 'Former ISI chief admits to

was filed against the alleged role of ISI in distributing funds to 'friendly' politicians by Air Marshall Asghar Khan (Retd) in 1996. On 19 October 2012, the Supreme Court tribunal found Aslam Baig and Asad Durrani guilty of violating the Constitution for their roles in the bribery.[8]

There were also stories that the conversation between the Indian prime minister Rajiv Gandhi and Benazir Bhutto was clandestinely recorded on 17 July 1989 by a Pakistani intelligence agency while the former was on a state visit to Pakistan. The room used for their private meeting was bugged. Apparently, among other issues, the two leaders discussed the possibility of mutual troop reduction to which Benazir agreed in principle. This was conveyed by the Chief of Army Staff General Aslam Baig to the then President Ghulam Ishaq Khan, which is believed to have led to their decision to topple the Benazir government.[9]

Fatima explained that given the unscrupulous use of multiple resources available to the establishment, including through the ISI, Benazir was left with little alternative. The ISI is a powerful institution in Pakistan. Benazir's survival in politics was dependent on mustering the required resources. Zardari did that for her, she said, without commenting on the truth behind the Mr 10 per cent allegation.

---

doling out money to Pak politicians', Press Trust of India, appearing in NDTV World on 9 March 2012.

[8] Owen L. Sirrs in his 2016 book *Pakistan's Inter-Services Intelligence Directorate: Covert Action and Internal Operations* (Routledge) provides a comprehensive study of Pakistan's Inter-Services Intelligence Directorate (ISI), including the rise of Pakistan-backed religious extremist groups in Afghanistan, India and Central Asia, concluding that the ISI's 'vast powers pose a formidable obstacle to the long-term viability of Pakistani democracy'; '1990 election was rigged, rules SC', *Dawn*, 19 October 2012.

[9] The details in this paragraph have been filled in through openly available information on the Internet.

The British journalist Owen Bennett-Jones, author of *The Bhutto Dynasty: The Struggle for Power in Pakistan*, explained in an article in the *Mumbai Mirror* on 16 October 2020 that during her second government, Benazir told an aide that $200–300 million was needed to go into an election to fund the candidates and secure their loyalty. While many of her advisers gave several suggestions, Asif Ali Zardari actually did something, proving himself to be a man she could rely on. Bennet-Jones concludes that it was Zardari's ability to understand what she needed and to do it without fuss or even discussion, which was the foundation of their relationship.

While there's no way that corruption can be justified, this was as good an explanation as one could have! I was reminded of the well-known Hindi saying, '*Lohe ko loha kaatta hai*', literally meaning 'only iron can cut iron', or in English, 'diamond cuts diamond'. Fatima's explanation was not an acceptance of the charges of corruption under Benazir. Rather, she was trying to highlight the corrupt and powerful system that Benazir had to survive against. While I could not agree with fighting corruption with corruption, I could neither dispute nor disagree with Fatima's fundamental point about the nefarious role of the Pakistan Army and the ISI in Pakistani polity.

The ISI and the army virtually held Pakistan in shackles, and have done so, one way or another, almost throughout Pakistan's history. I would sometimes wonder who was the bigger victim of their shenanigans, India, or the people of Pakistan? I was often convinced that the people of Pakistan were perhaps the biggest victims of their so-called defenders.

After two hours of a pleasant time and innocent conversation over some tea and snacks, I said goodbye to Fatima and her sister. We promised to see one another again next time we were in the same town.

As I came out of the house and walked towards my car, reality struck hard. Two intelligence agents, dressed intimidatingly in identical black trousers and black leather jackets, came out of the Toyota Corolla that had followed me and entered the house I had just exited. I realized that I had unleashed the Pakistani 'deep state' upon my innocent friends, who were probably harassed and intimidated for the purpose of my visit and the details of the conversation. I never found out as that turned out to be my last meeting with my friend Fatima.

7

Karachi Halwa

Ghanashyam often tells a story about Karachi and his favourite sweet called Karachi halwa. He always loved this colourful chewy, sugary sweet filled with dry fruits. When we landed in Karachi for the first time, it was his ambition to try out his favourite sweet in its place of origin.

During our first evening, while having dinner with some local friends, Ghanashyam casually asked about Karachi halwa and mentioned that it was his favourite sweet. To our surprise, none of the locals had heard of the sweet! 'Perhaps they did not like sweets,' we thought later. The next day was the same; no one had heard of Karachi halwa. Someone then suggested a visit to Karachi's famous sweets shop to look for the famous Karachi halwa.

The day after, some of our friends took Ghanashyam to the famous sweets shop. 'If it sells in Karachi, you'll certainly find it here,' one of them said as they entered the shop. Ghanashyam looked at the first display of sweets. There was no Karachi halwa. The same for the second display! Somewhat perplexed, he looked helplessly at his friends. 'There's another display, Bhai. Look at that one too. You may find it there,' said the friend. He was lucky the third time. There, at the end, was a tray filled with delicious-looking Karachi halwa! He looked at his friends triumphantly and pointing to the tray, said happily, 'See, this is Karachi Halwa!'

The friends came closer to look at the sought-after delicacy. Instead of being impressed, they burst out laughing. 'This?!' asked one of them, adding 'this is Bombay halwa!' The sweet that we had been enjoying as Karachi halwa was called Bombay halwa in Karachi!

So, where did the halwa originate? Karachi or Mumbai (Bombay)? The word 'halwa' is derived from the Arabic word 'Haluw' or 'sweet'. In Arabic, it is also used for 'pretty', for a pretty girl or a pretty sight. This would indicate that Karachi halwa's origin may be outside the boundaries of undivided India, perhaps Iran or the Arab world or even Türkiye. Traditional wisdom indicates, however, that the sweet originated in Karachi.

We were excited to visit Karachi for the first time. Our first drive out of the hotel took us to Clifton, the upscale and affluent neighbourhood of Karachi. The driver pointed out the Teen Talwar (Three Swords) monument and explained that the former prime minister Zulfikar Ali Bhutto had got it built as part of a plan to beautify Karachi. Listening to our bemused comments about the somewhat odd-looking structure, he explained that the monument represented the then symbol of Bhutto's political party, the PPP.

Immediately thereafter, the driver pointed towards Bhutto's house, 70 Clifton. 'This house is a landmark in Clifton,' explained the driver. Indeed, Zulfikar Ali Bhutto addressed many press conferences at 70 Clifton. His daughter, the late prime minister, Benazir Bhutto, and her mother, Nusrat Bhutto, were kept under house arrest for three years in this house. The bungalow was declared a 'sub-jail' at the time. The Movement for the

Restoration of Democracy, the longest-serving political alliance, was formed there in January 1981. Benazir addressed her famous press conference on her return to Pakistan in 1986[1] also from the same house and lived there before moving to Bilawal House. Asif Ali Zardari, her husband, built Bilawal House, and named it after their first son, Bilawal Bhutto Zardari. 70 Clifton became the house of Benazir's brother, Mir Murtaza Bhutto, and his family, which still lives there. On 20 September 1996, Mir Murtaza Bhutto was killed in a police encounter near his house. Though Benazir mourned her brother openly, this did not prevent accusations by the Opposition and others. Benazir's government was dismissed by President Farooq Leghari following 'months of domestic turmoil and dismal performance of the economy'.[2] Murtaza's death and corruption were also important factors. Zardari was indicted for Murtaza's murder. He was acquitted in 2008.[3]

70 Clifton is no longer the centre of PPP politics which has shifted, not far, to Bilawal House. At the time of our first visit to Karachi, these events were still very much a part of contemporary politics, having occurred in the recent past.

We realized that 70 Clifton was not the only place of interest in the neighbourhood, when the driver pointed in the general direction to his left and announced that the infamous Dawood

---

[1] Following the military coup by Gen. Zia-ul-Haq and the imposition of military rule, Benazir, and her mother, Nusrat Bhutto were arrested. Nusrat was released to get treatment for cancer, but Benazir was kept largely in solitary confinement and was released only in 1984. In December 1985, martial law was lifted in Pakistan and Benazir decided to return home. She arrived at Lahore Airport in April 1986, where she was greeted by a large crowd.

[2] Robert LaPorte, Jr., 'Pakistan in 1996: Starting Over Again', *Asian Survey*, Vol. 37, No. 2 (1997), pp. 118–25; President Leghari's Order of November 5, 1996, pakistani.org.

[3] Ishaq Tandu, 'SHC acquits Zardari in Murtaza murder case', *Dawn*, 10 April 2008.

Ibrahim lived there. The head of the mafia-style crime syndicate D-Company is wanted in India for charges that range from terrorist acts, murder and drug trafficking to targeted killings and extortion. Dawood's origins are in Mumbai, where he founded the D-Company in the 1970s. He was living in the poshest part of Karachi, and even an ordinary driver was aware of his address. The Pakistani authorities, however, denied knowledge of Dawood's whereabouts!

Finally, under pressure from the Financial Action Task Force (FATF), Pakistan issued a notification on 18 August 2020 listing 259 UN-designated terrorists and eighty-nine terror entities/ organizations. The list included the name of Dawood Ibrahim, with his different aliases, five passport numbers (including old and revoked Indian passports) and the address of his three properties in Karachi. This list was issued ahead of FATF review of Pakistan's compliance in fighting terror and money laundering and to demonstrate Pakistani commitment to fighting terrorism. Pakistan's move was aimed at impressing FATF and avoid being moved from FATF's 'grey list' to the dreaded 'blacklist'. Pakistan had been on the 'grey list' since June 2018. When the Pakistani notification was issued, FATF was due to make a final decision on whether Pakistan should be downgraded to the 'blacklist' or be made a 'high-risk jurisdiction'.[4] However, soon after issuing the list, Pakistan denied any acknowledgement on its part of Dawood Ibrahim's presence on its soil.[5]

At the time we lived in Pakistan, the Muttahida Qaumi Movement (MQM) was a strong force in Karachi. Its origins lay

---

[4] Geeta Mohan and Kamaljit Kaur Sandhu, 'Now, Pakistan denies presence of Dawood Ibrahim in Karachi, says media claims are baseless', *India Today*, 23 August 2020.

[5] Suhasini Haider, 'Pakistan denies Dawood Ibrahim's presence in its territory', *The Hindu*, 23 August 2020.

in the All Pakistan Mohajir Student Organisation (APMSO), the student organization founded by Altaf Hussain in 1978. APMSO evolved into the Mohajir Qaumi Movement in 1984. Its support base consisted of the Urdu-speaking immigrant community that had migrated to Pakistan from India at the time of Partition. The MQM replaced the word 'Mohajir' (immigrant or refugee) with 'Muttahida' (united) in 1997. It describes itself as a secular political party.

Our driver in Karachi seemed to be a staunch supporter of the MQM. He told us that the Movement was invincible in Karachi. 'If they put up a lamp post as their candidate, it would win in Karachi,' he claimed. Indeed, the MQM was the dominant political force and had strong mobilizing capability in Karachi in those days.[6]

Karachi was the first capital of Pakistan in 1947. It remained so till 1959, when it moved to Rawalpindi and finally to Islamabad in 1967. Most of the refugees from Punjab who moved from India to Pakistan in 1947, settled in west Punjab, across the border. The Muslim refugees from the rest of India, settled largely in Sindh. Being the capital of Pakistan, as well as its commercial port city, Karachi drew the newly arrived immigrants like a magnet. Many of the Urdu-speaking Mohajirs came to occupy positions in the bureaucracy, creating resentment within the local ethnic Sindhi community.

The founding of the MQM in the mid-1980s and its increasingly militant posture were also resented by the native Sindhis, who already felt aggrieved that the Urdu-speaking Mohajirs enjoyed a near monopoly over political and economic power in Karachi. With civil society missing under military rule,

---

[6] 'The Mohajir: Identity and politics in multiethnic Pakistan' (ORF Occasion Paper by Sushant Sareen and Kriti M. Shah) provides interesting details.

a fertile ground was available for conflict. The failure to integrate the incoming Mohajirs with the residents, worsened the existing situation. The entry of Pashtun migrants, particularly Afghan Pashtuns, from the NWFP to Karachi, added another dimension to an already potent situation, as they brought with them problems linked to narcotics and weapons trade, which had roots in the NWFP. Major clashes took place between the Mohajir and Pashtun communities during 1985–86.

Tensions erupted into conflict among different communities once the military dictator General Zia-ul-Haq lifted martial law in December 1985. Karachi became the scene of intense conflict that peaked in 1986. Riots also broke out in the cities of Quetta in the Balochistan Province and Hyderabad in Sindh. The clashes were fierce due to the widespread use of weapons.

During its initial struggle as a student movement, the MQM had reportedly taken on the heavily armed Islami Jamiat e-Talaba (IJT). It was said that the MQM acquired a large cache of AK-47s and eventually managed to tame the IJT, breaking the latter's hold over Karachi University. The MQM's armed wing is said to have gained expertise in street fighting and urban warfare. It slowly made inroads into powerful local bodies and finally became a part of the provincial government in 1991. In this position, it was alleged to have used extortion and coercion with government support to increase its influence.

Authorities, especially the Pakistan Army, were becoming increasingly uncomfortable with the MQM's growing influence in urban Sindh. It was alleged that it had turned into a de facto parallel government, a 'state within a state', with an adversarial approach towards the government in Islamabad.

The government called on the army to 'help restore law and order'. Operation Cleanup was launched in May 1992 after alleged MQM activists mistreated a couple of army officers in Karachi. The army soon handed over the operation to the paramilitary rangers. The crackdown involved a massive deployment of the army/rangers which pushed the MQM underground. However, the violent tactics used by the army to curb it, tremendously enhanced the support the MQM had from the ethnic Mohajir community.

Following the withdrawal of the army, Karachi witnessed a series of car bombings, riots and killings in mid-1994 and the summer of 1995. Our friends in Karachi recalled that the intensity of violence in those days was unprecedented even for Karachi, which had been witnessing sporadic ethnic and sectarian violence for years. By 1996, Karachi was in a virtual civil war between the Pakistani security forces and the MQM. The Pakistan Rangers reportedly believed that an 'elite corps' in the MQM's military wing carried out torture and murder without the approval or knowledge of the party's leadership.

MQM supporters believed that the crackdown on terrorists in Karachi during the Operation Cleanup of 1992 was targeted more towards MQM members. It forced Altaf Hussain, the party leader, into exile in London. MQM sympathizers believed that the excessive violence directed against the party was the reason behind the MQM's anti-state militancy. Those days, Altaf Hussain's fiery speeches on telephone from London would be broadcast on loudspeakers and heard with devoted attention by a large number of his followers in Karachi.

The operations in Karachi left thousands of Mohajir civilians dead. Human rights organizations reported growing evidence of the involvement of the rangers and police in human rights abuses, including beatings, extortion, disappearances, torture and extrajudicial executions of suspected militants in fake encounter killings of Mohajirs.[7] Amnesty International (AI), the

---

[7] The Mohajir Qaumi Movement (MQM) in Karachi, January 1995–April 1996, refworld.org

international human rights organization, laid the blame for the violence at the door of the Pakistani state, without absolving the 'armed groups' for their role. AI accused Pakistan authorities of carrying out torture, including rape, disappearances, extrajudicial killings, punitive destruction of homes, death in custody and arbitrary killings of militants, with virtual impunity.[8]

While the fate of the MQM would see several ups and downs over the years, what stayed with me was the sad reality of the Mohajirs themselves. Having struggled and suffered for the creation of the state of Pakistan, having left behind their homes, properties, belongings and often their loved ones, they remained aliens in Pakistan, isolated as 'immigrants' from the rest of the Pakistani society.

This was brought home by a very personal experience when I tried to contact a close friend of my family. The gentleman had been next-door neighbour to my aunt's family prior to Partition. He kept in touch with the family over the years during his annual visits to India. He made a special visit from Karachi to console the family on their bereavement at the death of my aunt's father. He promised my aunt and her siblings to be a standby for his departed friend.

When we were posted to Islamabad, it was my aunt's fervent request that we reach out to him and his family and show our family's affection for them. While in Karachi, we called the number given to us by my aunt and fixed a time to visit him the next day. We reached the house at the appointed time but were turned away from the gate itself with the excuse that the person in question was not around. It became obvious to us that the family had been intimidated by the security agencies and warned against meeting us.

---

[8] 'Pakistan: The pattern persists: torture, deaths in custody, extrajudicial executions and "disappearances" under the PPP government', Amnesty International, 1 January 1995.

What kind of a Pakistan did they create for themselves and the Muslims of India! I wondered. A country where the State was so suspicious of its 'Mohajir' citizens, that an old man could not even meet the relatives of his dear friends in India!

The disappointment of not meeting our family friend was more than compensated for during our next visit to Karachi, when we got a lifetime's opportunity to visit Mohenjo-daro, near Larkana, in Sindh province.

Located on the bank of the river Indus, it is the largest archaeological site from the ancient Indus Valley civilization that existed about 5000 years ago. It is regarded as one of the world's earliest major cities and a contemporary of ancient Egypt and Mesopotamia. As a middle-school student, I remember reading about the Indus Valley and Harappan civilizations as the first lessons in our history book on ancient Indian history. Though discovered after the excavation of Harappa in Punjab province of British India, Mohenjo-daro for 'mound of the dead' in Sindhi, is said to be the better preserved and more impressive.

A visit to Mohenjo-daro leaves one wondering if we really know history as we claim to know it. Mohenjo-daro was the largest city of the once-flourishing Indus Valley (also known as Harappan) Civilization that was spread across north-east Afghanistan to north-west India during the Bronze Age. It was discovered following large-scale excavations led by the British archaeologist Sir John Marshall after an Archaeological Survey of India (ASI) officer, R.D. Banerji, believed he saw a buried stupa in 1922.

Listed as a UNESCO world heritage site in 1980, Mohenjo-daro shows an amazing level of urbanization and sophisticated planning. It is known for its Great Bath, a large bitumen-lined pool for communal bathing. Mohenjo-daro is constructed on a planned grid-like layout. Buildings are spread over the vast city and constructed using sun-dried bricks. Well-laid-out roads, with covered drains running alongside, reveal an extensive sewage network that seemed to be widely available to all. Water from around 700 wells, one well for every three houses, supplied the drainage and bathing systems. The 'circular well' design, still in use, is credited to the Indus Valley.

Several objects and artefacts were found in the excavation. The most well-known include a soapstone figure of a dignified-looking seated male called the 'Priest-King', even though there was no evidence of priests or kings in Mohenjo-daro. This figure is with Pakistan. A bronze statuette dubbed the 'Dancing Girl', is in the National Museum, New Delhi. India also received a seal that bears the image of a seated, cross-legged figure surrounded by animals, interpreted by some scholars as a yogi, and by others as a three-headed 'proto-Shiva'. Other discoveries included seated and standing figures, copper and stone tools, carved seals, balance scales and weights, gold and jasper jewellery, and children's toys.

Seals, sculptures and artefacts from the Indus Valley have been found in Mesopotamia, evidence that people of the Indus Valley Civilization were actively trading with the people of Mesopotamia. The discovery of balance scales and weights hint at the existence of an organized system of trading that perhaps involved both goods and services like artisans for construction. Trade probably took place by sea, and most likely goods were taken by oxcart and riverboat to the sea.

The script of Mohenjo-daro has not yet been deciphered, so no one really knows what troubles the civilization faced, or the reasons why it was abandoned. Our guide expressed concern about the fast decline of the ruins due to the problems of salinity, humidity and rainfall. The conservation efforts by the authorities seem to have damaged rather than helped: 'But most of the attempts at conservation by the authorities have been so bad and so amateur they have only accelerated the damage.'[9]

---

[9] Aleem Maqbool, 'Mohenjo Daro: Could this ancient city be lost forever?', BBC News, 27 June 2012.

As we stood at the Great Bath and looked around us, we were wonderstruck that 5000 years ago, there existed this ideal city with complex planning, incredible architecture, and complex water and sewage systems, making it one of the most advanced urban settings anywhere. Many towns even today do not have the systematic layout or facilities that this place offered a few thousand years ago! Even as we were overwhelmed by the sheer scale and perfection of the city, it was the houses that seemed awe-inspiring, with their front and back entrances, interconnecting rooms, neat brick walls, and even a basic toilet and sewage outlet. Especially astonishing was the discovery that some homes were built on two storeys.[10]

Back in Islamabad, it was a sense of anti-climax to find that hardly anybody had even heard of Mohenjo-daro; none of my friends and acquaintances had visited it! As I read these lines by American-born freelance writer Samantha Shea, written about Mohenjo-daro[11]—'In the dusty plains of present-day Sindh in southern Pakistan lie the remains of one of the world's most impressive ancient cities that most people have never heard of'—I was sadly reminded of the smug faces of Pakistanis in Islamabad who had no idea of the jewel lying ignored and abandoned in the dusty belly of their country.

Visits to Karachi were always educative. Like Lahore, the city is home to many of Pakistan's intellectuals, be it writers, journalists or politicians. Karachi has been the home of Pakistan's major newspaper *Dawn*. The *Herald*, a monthly magazine published by the Dawn Media Group, was avidly followed by diplomats for its extensive coverage of politics and current affairs. It produced well-researched stories, many of them exclusive scoops. The *Herald*

---

[10] Ibid.

[11] Samantha Shea, 'Pakistan's lost city of 40,000 people', BBC Travels, 15 November 2022.

was known for its in-depth analyses and investigative reporting. Though it stopped publication in July 2019, those days, it was Pakistan's most widely read magazine and was published from Karachi. The *Herald* contributed to my enjoyment of my children's baseball matches; I did not understand the game, so I would read the latest issue of the *Herald* while the other children were playing. It was intellectually nourishing to meet the journalists and politicians living in Karachi.

One such person was Biyyathil Mohyuddin Kutty, better known as B.M. Kutty. A Malayali Muslim from the Malabar coast of Kerala, he was a member of the Communist Party of Pakistan (CPP) and was associated with many left and centre-left political parties. In an obituary published after Kutty's death, Pakistani journalist Beena Sarwar described him as 'a lifelong activist, trade unionist, political worker, peace monger, humanist'.[12] He was once asked by Prime Minister Zulfikar Ali Bhutto, 'Why did you come to Pakistan? Unlike the Biharis and the UP and Delhiwalas, you had no compulsion to leave that paradise called Kerala. It also has the politics of your liking. Then why did you give all that up and come here?'[13]

Kutty had a big smile and a deep and strong voice. But what stood out most was his genuine desire for peace between India and Pakistan. Kutty gave me the first lesson on the communist movement in Pakistan.

The CPP was first formed in India, when the Communist Party of India felt that the ground situation behoved a communist revolution in Pakistan. Syed Sajjad Zaheer, an Indian Urdu

---

[12] Beena Sarwar, 'The Humanist Who Was Pakistan's Malayali Comrade B.M. Kutty', Wire, 29 August 2019.

[13] Shekhar Gupta, 'An Indian's guide to Baloch nationalism, Pakistan's Left & death of Malayali named BM Kutty' | YouTube Episode no. 248, ThePrint.

writer and Marxist ideologue working in both countries prior to Independence, moved to newly created Pakistan and became a founding member of the CPP.

The CPP faced a major setback when it was banned in 1954. Kamran Asdar Ali, in his book *Surkh Salam*,[14] blames the setback on the actions of the party's founding father Sajjad Zaheer 'exposed' in the 'Rawalpindi Conspiracy Case', which ruined the party, dealing it a fatal blow from which CPP never recovered. The Rawalpindi conspiracy was an attempted coup against Pakistan's first prime minister, Liaquat Ali Khan, in March 1951, planned by Major General Akbar Khan, along with poet Faiz Ahmad Faiz, writer Sajjad Zaheer and others.

Pakistani journalist and author Nadeem F. Paracha takes a slightly more benign view of the role of the Communist Party and its sympathizers.[15] According to his version, when the CPP was active in organizing industrial workers and peasants for the purpose of creating a communist uprising, it tried to hasten the revolutionary process in Pakistan by 'unwittingly' getting involved in the ambitious plan of a military coup by Major General Akbar Khan, popular in the army and an admirer of Türkiye's Mustafa Kemal Atatürk. According to Paracha, Akbar Khan had befriended Sajjad Zaheer and some Marxist intellectuals and progressive poets (such as Faiz Ahmed Faiz), with whom he began to discuss his idea of pulling off a 'progressive-nationalist coup'. After recruiting some officers from the military and the police, Akbar approached his friends in the CPP and asked them to help him streamline his post-coup government through the CPP and the influence that the party had at the time overprogressive/leftist

---

[14] Kamran Asdar Ali, *Surkh Salam: Communist Politics and Class Activism in Pakistan 1947–1972*, OUP Pakistan, 2016.

[15] Nadeem F. Paracha, 'The rise and fall of the communist party of Pakistan', *Dawn*, 13 April 2014.

student groups, labour unions and the intelligentsia. However, in 1951, some officers that Akbar had recruited spilled the beans and Akbar's planned coup was nipped in the bud by the government and the military.

Akbar, his wife, poet Faiz Ahmed Faiz, and dozens of officers and CPP members (including Sajjad Zaheer) were arrested, tried and thrown in jail. The CPP was banned. Though initially given long jail terms, by the mid-1950s, they were pardoned. Most of the CPP leadership went underground.

B.M. Kutty explained the challenges faced by the CPP in the 1950s in a completely different context. He saw the banning of the CPP as a direct outcome of pressure from the US on Pakistan.

Following the end of World War II, the US and its Western allies were engulfed in a Cold War with the Soviet Union and its allies, the Eastern Bloc. By 1947, US President Harry S. Truman had adopted the hard-line policy of 'containment' against the Soviet Union. This policy was inspired by the writings of American diplomat George F. Kennan, who argued in his 'Long Telegram' (1946)[16] from Moscow and thereafter in an article in 1947 'The Sources of Soviet Conduct'[17] that the Soviet regime was inherently expansionist; its influence had to be 'contained' in areas of vital strategic importance to the US. The depiction of communism as a 'malignant parasite' that had to be contained by all possible measures, became the ideological foundation of the Truman Doctrine, Marshall Plan and National Security Act of 1947.[18]

---

[16] The Long Telegram was a secret report sent by the US Ambassador in the Soviet Union, George Kennan, to President Truman on 22 February 1946.

[17] Foreign Affairs (July 1947), see Digital History, digitalhistory.uh.edu

[18] Lubna Saif, 'Pakistan and SEATO', Pakistan Journal of History and Culture, Vol. XXVIII, No. 2 (2007), http://www.nihcr.edu.pk/latest_english_journal/pakistan_and_seato.pdf.

The Containment Doctrine underwent a hard-line transformation under President Dwight D. Eisenhower, who came to the White House after the US elections of 1952. US policy under Eisenhower and his Secretary of State John Foster Dulles was more aggressive: The policy of 'containment' was replaced by the policy of 'liberation'.

Pakistan could not remain immune to the anti-communist policy trends in the US. In May 1954, Pakistan signed the United States-Pakistan Mutual Defense Assistance Agreement with the US. It became a member of the Southeast Asia Treaty Organization (SEATO) later that year, along with the US, Britain, France, Thailand, the Philippines, Australia and New Zealand. A year later, it joined the Baghdad Pact, also known as the Middle East Treaty Organization (METO), another mutual defence organization, with Britain, Türkiye, Iran and Iraq. While not a member, the US remained closely associated with it. In 1958, when Iraq left this pact, it was renamed the Central Treaty Organization (CENTO). By signing these defence pacts, Pakistan became one of the first few allies of the American Power System in its war against communism.[19] Pakistan, thus, became a willing partner in the US's war against communism.

There is hidden irony behind these developments. Most US foreign policymakers of the era failed to distinguish indigenous third-world social revolutionaries and nationalists from Soviet communism. The US found cooperative partners—generals and bureaucrats—in the war against communism. They came to control affairs at the expense of democratic institutions and steered Pakistan towards Dulles's collective security pacts. A 'controlled democracy' (explained on the grounds of the masses being illiterate and needing further training), and an 'authoritarian regime' backed

---

[19] Ibid.

by the army, were the outcome. The 'Doctrine of Necessity'[20] was not long in coming. The champions of the free world showed that they were not above compromising democracy in the developing world to secure their strategic interest.[21] 'Pakistan's international supporters were ambivalent about democracy too. The American Agenda was clear: a pro-Western Pakistan, a stable Pakistan, prosperous Pakistan, and a democratic Pakistan were all desirable, but in that order.'[22] A pro-American leadership would, thus, seem to have been a higher priority than democracy itself.

The 1954 ban on the CPP was a major setback to communists in Pakistan. But the communist ideology did not die. Members of the CPP found that they could continue to function within other progressive parties like the Azad Pakistan Party and the National Awami Party (NAP).

Another setback for the leftists in Pakistan came when major political and ideological differences between the world's two great communist powers—the Soviet Union and China—emerged openly in the 1960s. Not unlike communists elsewhere, NAP also split into pro-Soviet and pro-China groups. In 1967, the pro-Soviet faction became NAP-Wali (the larger group) and the pro-China faction became NAP-Bhashani. Some of the pro-China members joined Zulfikar Ali Bhutto's PPP, while some others formed their own organizations, such as the militant Mazdoor Kissan Party (MKP), which was inspired by the beginning of the Maoist 'Naxalite' guerrilla movement in India and Mao's 'Cultural Revolution' in China. The MKP's movement was crushed in 1974.

---

[20] Used by the judiciary in Pakistan to justify coups against civilian governments by generals Ayub, Yahya, Zia and Musharraf.

[21] Lubna Saif, 'Pakistan and SEATO'.

[22] Stephen P. Cohen, *The Idea of Pakistan*, Vanguard Books, Lahore, 2005, p.56, as quoted by Lubna Saif in 'Pakistan and SEATO'.

Whether it was rule of the military dictator, General Ayub Khan, or that of democratic Zulfikar Ali Bhutto of the PPP, communists suffered attrition under both. In the 1970s, when the Balochistan Province faced a serious insurgency, leftists found the needle of suspicion pointed towards them by the federal government. The process of decimation of the communists was expedited during the rule of General Zia-ul-Haq and the US-backed 'jihad' against Soviet forces in Afghanistan. The CPP and its cadres suffered even further marginalization when in the late 1980s, the Soviet Union began to suffer from grave economic problems. This process reached a zenith, following the fall of the Berlin Wall in 1989 and the collapse of the Soviet Union in 1991.

Meeting B.M. Kutty was a major highlight of the visit to Karachi. His narrative of the rise and fall of communist ideology in Pakistan and the implications it had on Pakistan's polity and society, gave me a better understanding of the continuing rightwards tilt in Pakistan. Without any effective liberal and leftist forces to balance the ultra-conservative right-wing, Pakistan was left to the mercy of fundamentalist and extremist ideologies. The substantive 'decline of labour and class-based politics and the concurrent forceful emergence of a politics increasingly shaped by issues of ethnic, religious, and sectarian differences'[23] became a hallmark of contemporary Pakistan. The communist narrative failed to keep up with the post-cold war, post 9/11 international and domestic upheavals, causing the balance to tilt further rightwards. Over the years, the erosion in the social and political fabric due to the predominance of the extreme right would threaten to devour Pakistan.

---

[23] Kamran Asdar Ali, *Surkh Salam*.

8

Nuclear and Missile Tests

11 May 1998; 3.45 pm; Pokhran, Rajasthan. The world was stunned as India tested three nuclear devices. A few hours later, India's Prime Minister, Atal Bihari Vajpayee, conveyed to a surprised world that the country had become a nuclear weapon state. Two days later, on 13 May, India carried out two more tests.

The 1998 nuclear tests, commonly called Pokhran-II, consisted of five detonations on 11 and 13 May that year at the Pokharan range in the Thar desert, in Rajasthan. The first three detonations included one fusion bomb; the remaining four were fission bombs. The tests were assigned the code name 'Operation Shakti'.

India's first peaceful nuclear test[1] was carried out under the leadership of Prime Minister Indira Gandhi on 18 May

---

[1] India characterized the underground test of a plutonium implosion device as a 'peaceful nuclear explosion', or PNE. During the negotiations for a

1974, with the code name 'Smiling Buddha'; the tests were conducted on Buddha Purnima[2]. 'The Buddha has finally smiled' was the cryptic message after the test to Mrs Gandhi from Raja Ramanna, Director of India's premier nuclear research institute, BARC.

Pokhran-I was the first confirmed nuclear test by a country outside the five permanent members of the United Nations Security Council. The test was the outcome of nearly two years of preparation; scientists at BARC had reportedly been authorized to detonate an indigenously designed nuclear device in September 1972.

In 1998, India carried out nuclear tests at the same location (hence Pokhran-II), once again on the day of Buddha Purnima. The operation was conducted in high secrecy, which by itself is a fascinating story. Reports said that apart from Prime Minister Vajpayee and his Principal Secretary, Brajesh Mishra, only the then Home Minister, L.K. Advani, knew about it. Even Defence Minister George Fernandes and the Cabinet Committee on Security are said to have been informed only later. Work was carried out at night to avoid US spy satellites. Team members wore army uniforms to disguise themselves and bomb shafts

---

treaty on non-proliferation of nuclear weapons (NPT), at the Eighteen Nation Disarmament Committee (ENDC), between 1965 and 1968, the US argued that there is only a thin dividing line between a PNE device and a nuclear weapon and did not accept PNE as an integral part of the civilian nuclear energy application, though in the 1950s and 1960s, the superpowers had used nuclear explosive technology for developmental and industrial applications like civil engineering projects, deep sea mining and so on. (Karthik S.P. asked: What was the difference between the two nuclear tests that India conducted vide Operation Shakti and Operation Smiling Buddha? Manohar Parrikar Institute for Defence Studies and Analysis, Ask an Expert.)

[2] Purnima: full moon night. Buddha Purnima: celebration in honour of Gautam Buddha.

were dug under camouflage. Precaution was also taken to fly in nuclear devices from different parts of the country to avoid suspicion.

There was considerable jubilation in India after the nuclear tests of 1998. To vast majority of Indians, it represented an assertion of India's strength and power, even machismo. The code name for the tests—Operation Shakti—meaning strength and power, added to this sense of jubilation. A rise in nationalistic fervour was, thus, the instinctive reaction in India. The covert nature of the preparations, and the way these had been kept hidden from the all-seeing US satellites, added to the upsurge of national pride. The media reflected this.

The 1998 nuclear tests resulted in a variety of sanctions against India by several major states, including Japan and the US. International pressure had prevented Indian nuclear tests twice in the past. Former Indian President Venkataraman revealed that: 'All preparations for an underground nuclear test at Pokhran had been completed in 1983 when I was the defence minister. It was shelved because of international pressure and the same thing happened in 1995.'[3] The national discourse also included pacifist arguments that questioned the need and value of nuclear testing, and whether nuclear tests had contributed to strengthening India's security. These were, however, virtually drowned out by the overall reaction to the tests.

The reaction in Pakistan was the opposite. India's nuclear tests created waves of anxiety and concern there. The nuclear issue has been a symbol of national pride in Pakistan. Former prime minister Zulfikar Ali Bhutto famously said in the 1970s that Pakistanis had no choice but to get their own atom bomb

---

[3] 'The Indian and Pakistani Nuclear Tests: Levanthal Remarks at Carnegie Meeting', Nuclear Control Institute, 16 July 1998.

even if that required them to 'eat grass, (or) even go hungry'.[4] Thus, the vehement and strong reactions in Pakistan did not come as any surprise. There were furious reactions all around; from the government to the media, and the average person on the street, all seemed enraged. Numerous statements blamed India for instigating an arms race in the region.

Bitterly condemning the tests on 13 May, Pakistan's Foreign Minister, Gohar Ayub Khan, was quoted as saying that the Indian leadership seemed to 'have gone berserk'![5] The day after the first tests, he claimed in an interview that Pakistan was ready to conduct its own nuclear test; 'Pakistan is prepared to match India . . . We in Pakistan will maintain a balance with India in all fields.'[6]

Perhaps mindful of his country's dire economic situation, Prime Minister Nawaz Sharif was more circumspect. Though he vowed that his country would give a suitable reply to India, he tried to maintain some ambiguity about whether a test would be conducted in response, saying that Pakistan was 'watching the situation' and will 'take appropriate action'[7] for its security. He sought to mobilize the Islamic world in support of Pakistan and criticized India for nuclear proliferation.

There was pressure on Sharif from the US, including from the then US President, Bill Clinton, to desist from reacting to India's tests. In talks with Sharif, President Clinton, is reported to have offered a lucrative aid package. He sent high-level civic–military delegations led by Strobe Talbott and General Anthony

---

[4] Pakistan Nuclear Overview, Fact Sheet, 5 November 2019, nti.org.

[5] UNI, 'Indian leadership has gone berserk', Rediff on the net, 13 May 1998.

[6] UNI, 'Pakistan under increasing domestic pressure to reply in kind', Rediff on the net, 12 May 1998.

[7] Ibid.

Zinni to Pakistan to lobby against the tests. The US put together a 'package of carrots and sticks, incentives and disincentives', to keep Pakistanis from testing. The US Ambassador Thomas Winston Simons Jr carried, what was described as 'very substantial assurances from the United States' to Nawaz Sharif's residence, apparently just before the decision to test was made.[8]

Neither international pressure nor Pakistan's dismal economic situation could curb the Pakistani reaction. Sharif responded 'after 17 days of strenuous US efforts to back him off'. Simons believed that Sharif responded 'because he was convinced—and probably correctly—that if he did not explode the Pakistani weapons in response he'd be kicked out' of office by his own elites. Ambassador Simons claimed that Nawaz Sharif had 'no appetite for nuclear explosion' and had said to him, 'I wish we could drop these bombs into the Arabian Sea' but was under tremendous pressure from hawks in his nationalist government.[9]

Popular public opinion in Pakistan was in favour of the nuclear blasts. Ministers in the cabinet and ruling party leaders openly supported the tit-for-tat nuclear tests. Opposition leader, Benazir Bhutto, came out strongly in favour of Pakistan's atomic tests, and the Islamist parties fully supported them too. We heard stories of how prominent and respected political analysts had begged 'Mian Saab' (Nawaz Sharif) to respond to India's tests at an event. At a meeting organized by the Minister of Religious Affairs in Lahore on 21 May, Majid Nizami, the chief editor and owner of the newspaper chain that included Pakistan's most prominent Urdu paper, *Jang* and the popular English paper the *Nation*, reportedly

---

[8] 'Neither country was looking outside', interview by the then US Ambassador to Pakistan, Thomas Simons, to the Association for Diplomatic Studies and Training.

[9] Ibid.

screamed at Sharif, saying: 'If you don't explode (it), we're going to explode you.'[10]

The widespread anger against India found its way to the few Indians living in Islamabad: people working at the Indian High Commission. We had planned a diplomatic dinner at our residence in the middle of May. Invitations had gone out to several of our counterparts in other diplomatic missions weeks back. A few of my counterparts from the UN offices in Islamabad were also invited. Following India's nuclear tests, a groundswell of anti-India sentiment prevailed in Pakistan. A day before our dinner, I received a call from one of our invitees to convey their inability to join us for dinner due to some 'unexpected development'. This was soon followed by other guests, till it seemed that we may be left with hardly any guests at all. One UN diplomat even asked if we were going ahead with the dinner. Representatives of other countries, even at a junior level, felt the need to react in tandem with local sentiments!

Succumbing to the pressure of his supporters and the wider public opinion, Sharif authorized Pakistan's nuclear tests. These were carried out under the code name Chagai-I and II on 28 and 30 May 1998, respectively. Pakistan's six underground nuclear tests were conducted at the Chagai and Kharan test site in the Balochistan Province. The six blasts were clearly aimed at one-upmanship, to beat the five tests conducted by India. My Indian friend, Abha's gardener, told her smilingly the day after the sixth test, '*Madam, humne chheh phod diye hain*,' meaning, 'Madam, we have blasted six!'

The anger on the streets did not disappear after the Pakistani tests. While foreign diplomats were polite in avoiding us, the reaction on the streets had no such limitations of courtesy.

On the morning of 31 May, an Attache-level diplomatic officer in the High Commission was brutally assaulted in front of

---

[10] Ibid.

his residence in Islamabad as he was walking from his residence to the house of a colleague living in the neighbourhood. They used to 'regularly go together for morning walks. His attacker, a security guard at the residence of a local politician living in the neighbouring house, accosted him and beat him up with a long wooden lathi, without notice or provocation. The officer suffered serious injuries, including a head injury and fractures in both arms. The middle-aged officer had to be hospitalized. He was a quiet, polite and friendly person, rather small in build, totally unassuming.

The matter created a furore in the Indian Parliament, where the Minister of State for External Affairs, Vasundhara Raje Scindia, gave a statement. As per practice, the Pakistani high commissioner was summoned by the foreign secretary of India, a strong protest was lodged, and Pakistan was reminded of its responsibilities under the Vienna Convention and the bilateral code of conduct to provide security to the staff of the Indian High Commission and their families living in Islamabad. As expected, the Pakistani high commissioner expressed regret and responded that 'his government was providing security to Indian personnel in Islamabad, and that this incident was only an individual occurrence. He also assured that a full investigation would take place'.[11]

Even for a group of people like us, hardened by incidents of abductions, beatings, torture and interrogation of colleagues by Pakistani intelligence, the circumstances of this assault were very disturbing. The senseless and random assault, without any provocation, by someone who would have seen the officer and his wife walking the street for months, day in day out, was unnerving. It added to our overall sense of insecurity. Anyone anywhere could

---

[11] UNI, 'Parliament goes ballistic over attack on Indian diplomat', Rediff on the net, 1 June 1998.

be a target of random violence. This assault was unique even for the turbulent India–Pakistan relationship.

For the officer and his wife, the turmoil did not end with his physical recovery. Upon release from the hospital, he had to return to the same house. By then, his attacker was roaming freely in the city. One night, I received a panicky call at around 10 p.m.; the couple had heard footsteps on their terrace and the staircase outside. It was an independent house that could be easily accessed from outside. Ghanashyam and I immediately rushed to their house. We also called a security supervisor. That night, we posted an India-based security assistant at their house. Next morning, we decided to look for another house near the homes of other Indian officials. Fortunately, there was a house available next door to an apartment occupied by a younger staff member. It was smaller than his entitlement, but the couple was glad to be next door to a colleague. There were several other families from the Mission living on that street. We decided informally to try and create a semi-Indian neighbourhood in the future and look for houses and flats within walking distance of each other.

Pakistan's nuclear programme was not new; the development of nuclear weapons had started way back in the early 1970s. The late prime minister Benazir Bhutto said in an interview to VOA that her father, former prime minister Zulfikar Ali Bhutto, had told her from his prison cell that preparations for a nuclear test had been made in 1977. (Her father was hanged by General Zia-ul-Haq in 1979.) 'And I remember that he expected Pakistan to have its first nuclear test in 1976 - sorry, in August 1977.'[12] This was confirmed by Pakistan's top nuclear

---

[12] Benazir Bhutto's interview to VOA on 30 October 2009, 'Former Prime Minister Says Pakistan Had Nuclear Capability Long Before Nuclear Tests', https://www.voanews.com/a/a-13-2005-03-03-voa4/394834.html, (accessed 27 June 2024).

physicist, Samar Mubarakmand in an interview with Pakistani journalist Hamid Mir on the TV channel, Geo News in March 2004. Mubarakmand said that the Pakistan Atomic Energy Commission (PAEC) had developed the design of an atomic bomb in 1978 and had successfully conducted a cold test after building the first atomic bomb in 1983.[13]

At the time of carrying out its nuclear tests, Pakistan's economy was grappling with ten years of economic mismanagement. A 1998 report of the Economist Intelligence Unit concluded that: 'Economic mismanagement, fiscal profligacy, rising bank defaults and high levels of corruption in the last ten years' had 'played havoc with Pakistan's economy . . . On the eve of Pakistan's nuclear test, the economy was already only limping along'.[14] Its external debt amounted to $32 billion. Sixty per cent of the government's revenue was going towards servicing Pakistan's total debt. Analysing the impact of the 1998 sanctions, Daniel Morrow and Michael Carriere wrote that:

> In October 1997, the government of Nawaz Sharif had reached an agreement with the IMF for an economic reform program supported by an IMF credit of $1.56 billion, to be disbursed in three tranches, and by a World Bank adjustment loan. As of April 1998, $1.2 billion of the IMF funds remained un-disbursed. Pakistan needed these funds to shore up its weak external position. In April 1998, it had foreign exchange reserves of only $1.4 billion. These were enough for just about 90 days of imports. Pakistan, thus, needed about

---

[13] Text of the interview has been put on the web by asadasif.com as My little world: Separating facts from myths, Pakistan's nuclear programme.

[14] Economist Intelligence Unit, Country Report on Pakistan, Third Quarter, 1998.

$2 billion in net in-flows in 1998 to avoid loss of reserves and /or reduced imports.[15]

It was also known that the US would impose sanctions under its Glenn amendment[16] following the nuclear tests and that other Western nations would do likewise. Pakistan was already under US sanctions imposed by the 1985 Pressler Amendment[17] due to which no bilateral aid flows existed to be cut under the Glenn Amendment. While the loss of US bilateral assistance was not a factor following the May 1998 tests, the sanctions would have much wider implications. To start with, fourteen countries, including Japan, Germany, Australia, Canada, Denmark and Sweden, suspended bilateral aid programmes, though only the Japanese sanctions involved significant amounts as Japan suspended all loans to Pakistan totaling $231 million in 1997–98, and cancelled grant aid of approximately $55 million.

Following the nuclear tests, the US and other shareholders in the International Monetary Fund (IMF) formed a coalition to block disbursement of the IMF credit and the parallel adjustment

---

[15] Daniel Morrow and Michael Carriere, 'The Economic Impacts of the 1998 Sanctions on India and Pakistan', *Nonproliferation Review*, Fall 1999.

[16] Legislation sponsored by former Democratic Senator from Ohio, Senator John Glenn. The Glenn Amendment refers to an amendment to the Arms Export Control Act of 1994 (Section 102). It states that the US must oppose (vote no or abstain) any IFI loan or financial or technical assistance that does not directly support basic human needs (BHN) when a non-nuclear weapon state detonates a nuclear explosive device—it requires the US President to impose seven sanctions.

[17] The Pressler Amendment banned most economic and military assistance to Pakistan unless the US President certified on an annual basis that 'Pakistan does not possess a nuclear explosive device and that the proposed United States assistance program will reduce significantly the risk that Pakistan will possess a nuclear explosive device.'

loan from the World Bank. The expectation that the sanctions would block the ongoing IMF support caused a collapse of market confidence, which affected the capital flows, the exchange rate and the aggregate gross domestic product (GDP) growth in Pakistan. New private inflows virtually stopped. Foreign exchange reserves fell to extremely low levels. The G-7 countries, and several non-G-7 nations, joined the US in opposing new non-humanitarian lending by the IMF, the World Bank and the Asian Development Bank to Pakistan (and India). As it turned out, the delay of the IMF support package hampered Pakistan's effort to receive financial support from the Arab world: a $1.5 billion rescue package, consisting of funds from Arab private banks and financial institutions and arranged by the Islamic Development Bank (IDB).[18]

The strong anti-India sentiment prevalent in Pakistan at the time, coupled with the dire economic situation, made me uneasy. I decided to withdraw our small foreign currency savings held in our bank account in Islamabad. This represented our net worth at the time. One of the Indian journalists also withdrew his money in time. Due to the fear of unauthorized entries into Indian homes in Islamabad, he kept a sealed envelope in my almirah in the office, where I had also kept my own family's savings.

Immediately after Pakistan's nuclear tests, on 28 May 1998, perhaps to avoid a post-test run on its banks, especially foreign currency, the government froze all foreign currency accounts in Pakistan.[19] While immediately putting an end to remittances from

---

[18] Daniel Morrow and Michael Carriere, 'The Economic Impacts of the 1998 Sanctions on India and Pakistan', *Nonproliferation Review*, Fall 1999.

[19] This economically unsound act of freezing foreign currency accounts took place just hours after Pakistan's nuclear tests. The Pakistani press reported that the government took this step believing that the blasts, along with the sanctions that would follow, would cause massive investor flight. Other

Pakistanis overseas, a major source of net inflows, this decision caused considerable difficulty to Pakistan-based offices of foreign newspapers and companies, which depended on remittances from their headquarters. The ruling was not applicable to diplomats, but one of the two Indian journalists in Pakistan had to borrow to survive till a special provision was created by the Pakistan government to deal with the anomaly.

For Pakistan's economy, the nuclear tests and their aftermath were a catastrophe heaped on a disaster! The signs were everywhere. The market rate for the Pakistani rupee depreciated by 28 per cent from Pak Rs 45 to the dollar in early May to Pak Rs 63 in mid-July 1998. It remained 16 per cent below its pre-test value even after most of the sanctions had been lifted. Eventually, the Government of Pakistan devalued the official currency rate by 4.2 per cent on 28 June 1999.[20]

Pakistan's projected GDP growth rate was revised downwards from 6 to 3.1 per cent by the government, though some believed that even this was optimistic, and a GDP growth rate of 1.6 per cent was more likely.[21]

The Karachi Stock Exchange (KSE) crashed approximately by 15 per cent on 1 June, when it opened after the nuclear tests, its worst-ever performance. It fell another 13 per cent over five days after the official announcement of the US sanctions on 18 June. On 10 July, the Pakistani daily newspaper the *Nation* ran a story that quoted IMF Middle East Director Paul Chabrier

---

reports indicated that Sharif froze all currency accounts to counter the negative financial effects of the sanctions by keeping as much currency in Pakistan as possible. Mohammad Uzair, 'Continuous depreciation of Pak rupee', *Dawn* (Pakistan), 24 August 1998.

[20] Daniel Morrow and Michael Carriere, 'The Economic Impacts of the 1998 Sanctions on India and Pakistan', *Nonproliferation* Review, Fall 1999.

[21] Economist Intelligence Unit, Country Report on Pakistan, 1 June 1999.

as saying that the G-8 countries had the last word on IMF funding to Pakistan. On that same day, the KSE reached a then all-time low of 777.26. Three days later, it was reported that the postponement of IMF funding had led to 'the blackest week' in the history of the KSE.[22]

Relations between India and Pakistan hit a new low following the nuclear tests in 1998. A new context was added to the already murky picture as Pakistan started to project South Asia as a 'nuclear flashpoint', linking the 'unresolved Kashmir question' to the flashpoint.

The post nuclear test flashpoint narrative gained new strength within a year as both countries went through a round of missile tests.

On 11 April 1999, we were at the home of our dear friends, Safina and Raja, in Lahore. Their daughter, Shaheen, had been admitted to the prestigious Lahore University of Management Sciences (LUMS).[23] 'I am really enjoying my time at LUMS, Ruchi aunty,' said Shaheen as we sat on the edge of the bed in the master bedroom watching the news on TV. It was a matter of pride for Shaheen to have been accepted in Pakistan's topmost educational institution. I was happy for this recognition of her talent. As we sat chatting amiably, our attention was drawn to the news when the newsreader announced that India had tested its medium-range ballistic missile, Agni-II, capable of carrying nuclear warheads with a range of over 2000 km!

---

[22] 'G8 has last word on ESAF revival, warns IMF director', *Nation* (Pakistan), 10 July 1998; 'The blackest week in history of KSE', *Nation* (Pakistan), 13 July 1998.

[23] LUMS was set up by a well-known Pakistani businessman in 1983. In 2020, it was ranked no. forty globally in the 'World's Best Small Universities' by Times Higher Education—the only Pakistani university to figure on the list.

Suddenly, it was as if the bubble of comfortable trust and camaraderie that had enveloped us, was shattered. Shaheen's head jerked in my direction, and I saw a clear expression of hurt mixed with betrayal in her eyes as if she had only at that moment realized that she was sitting not with a friend but the representative of an enemy country! I tried to reassure her by saying that with a range of 2000 km, the missile was not aimed at Pakistan and that being a large country, India's security challenges went beyond Pakistan. That seemed to calm her anxiety, but the atmosphere was not the same again. We soon decided to join the others.

To the average Pakistani, it did not really matter that statements coming out of India were restrained and lacked belligerence. In his address to the nation, Prime Minister Vajpayee said that the test was not meant for aggression against any nation and was 'a purely defensive step'.[24] Other statements from India also emphasized that Agni-II was not a threat to any country, including Pakistan, and was only aimed at strengthening India's defence capabilities. However, repeated Indian assertions that Agni-II was not 'Pakistan-centric' did not mean much to the average person and did little to alter the perceptions in Pakistan.

The response of the Pakistani government reflected this Pakistani perception. Prime Minister Nawaz Sharif promised 'a necessary response to India's continuing provocative actions'.[25] Pakistani statements, including by the Chief of the Army Staff General Pervez Musharraf, were clear that Pakistan would respond by test-firing its own missiles to 'restore parity'. Pakistanis also blamed India for triggering another arms race in

---

[24] Raj Chengappa, 'Pakistan's reply to India's testing of Agni-II intensifies deadly nuclear missiles race', *India Today*, 26 April 1999; 'Agni-II successfully test-fired', Rediff.com, 11 April 1999, based on UNI report.

[25] Raj Chengappa, 'Pakistan's reply to India's testing of Agni II intensifies deadly nuclear missiles race', 26 April 1999.

the subcontinent. On 11 April, Pakistani Foreign Minister Sartaj Aziz said the Defence Committee of the Cabinet (DCC) would meet to discuss Pakistan's response to India's test firing of its Agni-II intermediate-range ballistic missile (IRBM). Aziz said that the DCC would consider all aspects (including that Agni-II has a range of 2000 km) before test-firing one or two of the Shaheen-1, Shaheen-2 or Ghauri-2 missiles.[26]

Pakistan's response to the testing of Agni-II by India came barely three days later. On 14 April, Pakistan test-fired the Ghauri-2 missile from a site near Jhelum city in north-east Pakistan. It was reported to have struck a target in the Balochistan desert about 1100 km away, though Pakistan claimed that Ghauri-2 had a potential range of 2300 km. Another test of Shaheen ballistic missile, the next day, with a range of 800 km seemed to calm the turbulence as a Pakistani Foreign Office statement said that the Shaheen ballistic missile test had concluded for the time being.[27]

India's tests were seen in Pakistan as being detrimental to the peace and security of the region and of having started a missile and nuclear arms race on the subcontinent. It was also said that the testing was done in the last days of the Vajpayee government in India. But a look at India's gradually worsening security situation in the 1990s provides a better context for the tests.

Indian analysts had, for some time, been concerned about Chinese nuclear and missiles proliferation to Pakistan. Reports about mutual proliferation between Pakistan and North Korea added to India's insecurities. In a testimony before the US Senate Select Committee on Intelligence on 22 February 1996, John

---

[26] 'Pakistan Completes Preparations for Missile Test', Pakistan Institute for Air Defence Studies, PIADS Pakistan Defense News Bulletin, April 1999.

[27] 'Pakistan Conducts Second Nuclear Capable Missile Test', CNN, 15 April 1999; 'Pakistan Conducts 2nd Missile Test', New York Times, 15 April 1999.

M. Deutch, the director of Central Intelligence,[28] had confirmed earlier reports that Pakistan had taken delivery of sensitive nuclear technology used to develop weapons-grade uranium. He also confirmed that Pakistan had received M-11 ballistic missiles from China.[29] According to a report,[30] US intelligence agencies had concluded that Pakistan had deployed nuclear-capable Chinese M-11 missiles and that the transfer was part of a conspiracy to skirt missile-control agreements. It added that the declaration, contained in interagency intelligence reports produced in May 1996, confirmed for the first time that Pakistan had a strategic nuclear delivery capability. Similar reports were carried by the Indian media as well.

Pakistan was widely believed to have received the blueprints for a 1966 design of a U-235 nuclear-implosion device from China in the early 1980s. This device could be used as a missile warhead and was reported to weigh about 1300 kg, with a yield of 12–25 Kt. Pakistan also signed a deal with China in 1989 to purchase thirty-four solid-fuelled M-11 ballistic missiles, which could deliver a 500-kilogram payload over 300 km.[31] A CIA report to the US Congress said that Chinese entities had been the principal suppliers for Pakistan's serial production of solid-

[28] 17th Director of Central Intelligence in office from 10 May 1995–15 December 1996

[29] Details available in Senate statement of 12 June 1996, US Senator Larry Pressler, available in Congressional Record, under title 'Chinese Nuclear Missiles in Pakistan', p. S6139.

[30] Bill Gertz, 'Pakistan Deploys Chinese Missiles', *Washington Times*, 12 June 1996.

[31] 'Pakistan and North Korea dangerous counter-trades', Vol. 8, No. 9, November 2002, paper by the International Institute for Strategic Studies for Carnegie Endowment.

propellant short range ballistic missiles (SRBMs) such as the Shaheen-1 and Haider-1[32].

The warhead design received from China, was too large (1300 kg instead of 500 kg) to be carried on an M-11. With a range of 300 km, the M-11 also did not have the range to threaten New Delhi; nor could it threaten large population centres beyond India's Thar desert. Pakistan's search for an appropriate delivery system that could carry heavy nuclear warheads beyond Thar desert led to the purchase of approximately 12–25 liquid-fuelled No-dong ballistic missiles from North Korea. The No-dong system could deliver a payload of 700–1000 kg over 1000–1300 km.[33]

Nuclear-missile links between Pakistan and North Korea are thought to go back to the early 1990s. Pakistani officials are said to have visited North Korea way back in 1992 to view a No-dong prototype. In May 1993, Pakistani engineers and scientists reportedly attended the No-dong test-launch at Musudan-ri, the North Korean rocket launching site, Tonghae Satellite Launching Ground.[34]

In 1996, Taiwanese officials seized 15 tons of ammonium perchlorate[35] on a freighter bound from North Korea to Pakistan's Space and Upper Atmosphere Research Committee. In June 1999, acting on an intelligence tip-off, customs officials in India, seized the North Korean ship *Ku Wol San* at Kandla in Gujarat. The ship's manifest listed water purification equipment, but a search revealed it to be carrying missile components and metal

---

[32] T.V. Paul, 'Chinese–Pakistani Nuclear/Missile Ties and the Balance of Power', *Nonproliferation Review*, Summer 2003.

[33] 'Pakistan and North Korea dangerous counter-trades', Vol. 8, No. 9, November 2002, paper by the International Institute for Strategic Studies for Carnegie Endowment.

[34] Ibid.

[35] An oxidizing agent used in most modern solid-propellant formulas.

casings to Pakistan, along with twenty-two technical manuals for Scud-type ballistic missiles.[36]

Increased frequency of cargo flights between North Korea and Pakistan was also suspicious. From late-1997 onwards, about three flights a month increased to around nine in January 1998. The curtain was finally lifted with the testing of a No-dong, christened Ghauri, by Pakistan in April 1998. Viewing it as a violation of the Missile Technology Control Regime (MTCR), the US State Department imposed sanctions on Pakistan's Khan Research Laboratories and North Korea's Ch'anggwang Trading Company.[37] Former prime minister Benazir Bhutto confirmed in an interview to VOA in October 2009 that she did get missile technology from North Korea, but that Pakistan paid cash for it.[38]

These reports and the testing of Ghauri missile in 1998 were a clear sign of Pakistan developing the capability to deliver nuclear warheads to targets across much of India. Pakistan's ability to threaten India's heartland was a breach of India's strategic redlines. This concern was subsequently highlighted in a statement to the Indian Parliament on 15 December 1999, by the then Indian Foreign Minister Jaswant Singh that China and North Korea were helping Pakistan with its missile program including missile technology, missile components, and liquid fuel, adding that Pakistan's Ghauri missile was a copy of North Korea's No-dong ballistic missile, and that China had supplied

---

[36] Gaurav Kampani, 'Second Tier Proliferation: The Case of Pakistan and North Korea', *Nonproliferation Review*, Fall-Winter 2002.

[37] 'Pakistan and North Korea dangerous counter-trades', Vol. 8, No. 9, November 2002, paper by the International Institute for Strategic Studies for Carnegie Endowment.

[38] 'Former Prime Minister Says Pakistan Had Nuclear Capability Long Before Nuclear Tests', voanews.com, 30 October 2009.

Pakistan with M-11 missiles in addition to components and technology related to M-11 production.[39]

India's testing of the Agni-II IRBM conducted on 11 April 1999 needs to be seen in the changed context of nuclear and missile proliferation taking place around the country, making India vulnerable from more than one direction.

The international community invariably overlooked the changes in India's security paradigm. Alarmed by the nuclear tests conducted by India and Pakistan, the international community urged both countries to resolve all outstanding disputes to avoid a nuclear conflict. The UN Security Council resolution 1172 adopted on 6 June 1998 urged India and Pakistan to remove tension and to find solutions of irritants, including Kashmir. The US and the G-8 countries also tried to push for bilateral talks to avoid any threat of war.

After the tests of Agni-II by India and Ghauri-2 and Shaheen missiles by Pakistan, official voices from powerful countries reacted in an 'even handed' manner. If anything, India was expected to be magnanimous in understanding the security concerns of its smaller neighbour, overlooking that others were aiding Pakistan's nuclear and missile programmes, also ignoring the threat posed to India by a much larger and powerful neighbour—China.

Following India's missile tests, a spokesperson for the Pakistani Foreign Office said that India was not amenable to concluding a strategic restraint regime agreement with Pakistan; claiming that such an agreement had acquired 'greater validity' after the tests of ballistic missiles and that the 'restraint regime' was intended to define 'the minimum deterrence, both nuclear and conventional' required for the security of the two countries.

---

[39] 'PRC, DPRK Missile Sales to Pakistan', NapsNet Daily Report, 15 December 1999; 'Pakistan Getting Missile Technology from China, North Korea: Minister', AFP, 15 December 1999.

While making such proposals, Pakistan equated its own security situation vis-à-vis India, with those of India's larger security concerns. It also ignored its own nuclear and missile proliferation. As a large country, situated in a challenging geographic location, India must contend with a far more complex security environment than Pakistan.

Understandably, the average person in Pakistan did not comprehend the complexity of the security situation in South Asia. As a result, tensions on the street during such periods became tangibly higher. Life could become oppressive in Islamabad during such times!

9

Dialogue, Friendship and a Visit to Lahore

'The relationship between India and Pakistan can be good, it can be bad; it can never be normal,' said a former foreign secretary of Pakistan to Ghanashyam, a few months before our departure from Brussels, where we were posted before moving to Islamabad. He was visiting his daughter in Belgium. The events of 1998–99 frequently reminded us of his wise words.

The deterioration in the atmosphere following the nuclear tests of 1998 was visible on both sides. It was clear that things could not continue along the same trajectory indefinitely. Both sides were also under pressure from an international community worried about the increasing bitterness between two nuclear-armed, traditionally inimical neighbours.

A meeting between the Indian prime minister Vajpayee and his Pakistani counterpart Nawaz Sharif at New York in September 1998 signalled a softening of the atmospherics. The initiative at New York on the margins of the United Nations General Assembly led to the announcement of the setting up of a Composite Dialogue on eight subjects. It was hoped that the Composite Dialogue would build trust and confidence, develop mutually beneficial cooperation, and help to address outstanding issues. The aim was to move bilateral relations forward over a broad front to achieve robust progress. All subjects were to receive equal significance and 'addressed substantively and specifically through the agreed mechanism in an integrated manner'.[1]

The Composite Dialogue started with foreign secretary-level talks between India's foreign secretary, K. Raghunath and his Pakistani counterpart, Shamshad Ahmad in Islamabad on 15–18 October 1998. They held separate meetings on the agenda items, which included peace and security, including confidence-building measures, and Jammu and Kashmir. In the absence of any positive outcome, the holding of the foreign secretary-level talks in Islamabad was by itself seen as progress.

An unexpected development during the visit of the Indian delegation exposed the deep roots of Islamization in Pakistan. On 17 October 1998, Maulana Muhammad Abdullah, a well-known Pakistani Islamic scholar and the first Imam of Lal Masjid (Red Mosque), was assassinated. Before the construction of the

---

[1] Joint Statement issued on 23 September 1998 following the meeting of foreign secretaries of India and Pakistan. All outstanding issues were to be dealt with at the levels indicated below:
(i) Peace and Security including CBMs—Foreign Secretaries
(ii) Jammu and Kashmir—Foreign Secretaries
(iii) Siachen—Defence Secretaries
(iv) Wullar Barrage/Tulbul Navigation—Secretaries, Water & Power
(v) Sir Creek—Additional Secretary (Defence)/Surveyors General
(vi) Terrorism and Drug Trafficking—Home/Interior Secretaries
(vii) Economic and Commercial Cooperation—Commerce Secretaries
(viii) Promotion of friendly exchanges in various fields—Secretaries, Culture

landmark Faisal Mosque, Lal Masjid was the only Central Mosque of Islamabad and used to be visited regularly by the late President Zia-ul-Haq. Lal Masjid remained an important religious centre of the capital even after completion of the Faisal Mosque. President Zia was said to have wanted Maulana Abdullah to be the first Imam of the Faisal Mosque, an offer that the Maulana apparently did not accept.

The assassination happened in broad day light, at noon, right in front of the Maulana's house. As he got out of his car, a man standing in front of the door walked towards him, pulled out a gun and opened fire, emptying the magazine. He also fired at the Maulana's elder son. Maulana succumbed to his injuries on the way to the hospital, while his son escaped death. An accomplice in a car waiting outside assisted the assassin's escape.

Maulana Abdullah was well known. He was credited with founding the Jamia Faridia (later Faridia University). He was known as the person who introduced a female madrassa education system in Pakistan by creating Jamia Hafsa, Pakistan's first female seminary. Lal Masjid was known for the role it played in recruiting and training the Mujahideen to fight the Soviet troops along with the Afghan Mujahideen during the Soviet Afghan War (1979–89). A few months before his assassination, Maulana Abdullah was reportedly a part of a delegation that went to Afghanistan and met the Taliban leader, Mullah Omar, Al-Qaeda founder Osama Bin Laden and the second Amir of Al-Qaeda Ayman Al Zawahiri.

The assassination of such a prominent cleric right outside his house was shocking. All of us were shaken as we regularly shopped at the Aabpara market located near Lal Masjid. A Pakistani friend suspected the hand of the ISI, and sectarian differences within it, for the killing. In response to my shocked scepticism, she said, 'Why? Don't you think these differences exist within the ISI?'

This suspicion was strengthened when rumours emerged that the family was having to make considerable efforts to have the case investigated. Apparently, the man who was arrested and even identified by an eyewitness during the identity parade was released the next day without reason.

The insinuations against the ISI or stories of police inaction, could have been the outcome of the fevered imagination of my friend, but it was a strange coincidence that the assassination coincided with the first round of composite dialogue in Islamabad.

This was my first experience of India–Pakistan foreign secretary-level talks. The Mission had been reporting on some of the political developments over the past several months. Of particular interest had been the visit of Mushahid Hussain to the camp of the terrorist outfit, Lashkar-e-Taiba[2] (LeT), on 17 April, just six months before the talks.[3] He was then Pakistan's information minister in the Nawaz Sharif government. The Governor of the Punjab province, Shahid Hamid, and other officials were with him for the outfit's annual event. This was the first-ever public visit by a cabinet minister to the LeT camps. Reports of the visit of the federal information minister and the Punjab Governor had been carried in sections of the Pakistani media, and photographs of these dignitaries on the podium with the LeT leader, Hafiz Saeed, had been in circulation.

Located at Muridke, 30 km from Lahore, the LeT camp had been set up in 1987 allegedly with the objective of providing covert support to anti-India insurgency, especially in Jammu and Kashmir, and mounting insurgency operations in both Afghanistan and Kashmir. As per reports of past events, chilling tales of killings of Indian soldiers had been narrated by Kashmir-

---

[2] 'Army of the pure' is the armed wing of the Markaz-e-Dawat-ul Irshad. It is a Pakistan-based Wahabi group mainly fighting India in Jammu and Kashmir.

[3] Ramesh Vinayak and Manoj Joshi, 'Islamic radical groups espouse jehad as a way of life', *India Today*, 7 September 1998.

returned cadres. The LeT had training facilities in the Kunar Province of Afghanistan. LeT fighters, along with Hizb-ul-Mujahideen militants, had been killed in August 1998, when US cruise missiles had struck Osama bin Laden's training camps in Afghanistan.[4]

The LeT is believed to be one of the organizations trained by the Pakistan Army and its chief intelligence agency, the ISI, during the time of Pakistan President Zia-ul-Haq. Starting with attacks on Hindus and Sikhs in India in its early years, the LeT has been accused of attacking various military and civilian targets in India over the years, including the 2001 attack on the Indian Parliament, the 2008 Mumbai attacks and the 2019 Pulwama attack on the Indian armed forces.

In a paper for Carnegie Endowment, Ashley J. Tellis, specialist in international security issues, highlights Pakistani state support for the LeT. He quotes Hafiz Mouhammed Saeed, the LeT chief, as wholeheartedly endorsing the objective of destroying India, as he asserted in an interview in 1999 that 'jihad is not about Kashmir only . . . Today, I announce the break-up of India . . .'[5]

Following the terrorist attacks on New York's 'twin towers' on 11 September 2001, Pakistan came under pressure from the US to crack down on such militant groups. It also faced the prospect of war with India, after Indian troops were mobilized on the Pakistan border following the terrorist attack on India's Parliament in December 2001. In the face of this dual pressure, Pakistan decided to ban LeT in January 2002 and arrested its

---

[4] A senior al-Qaeda official was captured in a Lashkar-e-Taiba safe house in Pakistan in March 2002. The outfit is designated as a terrorist organization by India, the US, the UK, the European Union, Russia, Australia, the United Nations (under the UNSC Resolution 1267 Al-Qaeda Sanctions List) and even Pakistan.

[5] Ashley J. Tellis, 'The Menace that is Lashkar-e-Taiba', Carnegie Endowment for International Peace, March 2012.

leader, Hafiz Muhammad Saeed; he was released a few months later. To evade scrutiny, Hafiz Saeed established the Jamaat-ud-Dawa (JUD), with its charity organization called the Falah-e-Insaniyat Foundation. It was immediately apparent that this was a front for the LeT. When the Pakistani government banned JUD in February 2019, after the Pulwama attack in India, the names were once again changed to Al Madina and Aisar Foundation, respectively. Both continued to act as before. Though these developments happened much after the foreign secretary-level talks of 1998, the LeT was already notorious by then.

When India's foreign secretary drew attention during the Composite Dialogue, to the growing terrorist violence in Jammu and Kashmir by the LeT and referred to the visit of high-level Pakistan government dignitaries to the camp of this group, I naively expected the Pakistani delegation to, at the very least, look a little embarrassed or concerned. I was amazed to see that it was water off a duck's back. Pakistan's Foreign Secretary Shamshad Ahmad claimed that he was not even aware of the existence of such an organization in his country! This assertion was bizarre in view of the highly publicized visit to the headquarters of the LeT at Muridke by the then Governor of Punjab, Shahid Hamid, and the then Information Minister, Mushahid Hussain.

I saw Pakistan's brazen reaction as hypocrisy of the Pakistani government. I remember wondering about the purpose of talks in such a situation, thinking to myself in amazement, 'How can Pakistan expect India to have any serious discussions on Jammu and Kashmir or any other issue, in the face of such brazenness!'

The differences between the two sides came out into the open at the press conference on the final day of the talks. Both foreign secretaries made no effort to conceal the difference in approach and divergent positions taken by them on behalf of their respective countries. India's position had long been to proceed from easy to difficult issues. The trust and goodwill generated by finding solutions to simpler issues helps to build the confidence to take on more ticklish and difficult issues. India's foreign secretary, K. Raghunath explained this, saying 'It does not generally help in international relations to front-load a process with problems that are unduly complicated. This is a basic common sense idea.'

Pakistan's 'single-agenda approach' was the main roadblock. The commonly used English idiom, 'one trick pony' best describes this approach. A 'Kashmir only' approach and attitude has never been acceptable to India.

Following the 1998 nuclear tests, Pakistan's propaganda machine had started drumming the 'Kashmir is a nuclear flashpoint' narrative. Raghunath used the visit to dismiss this theory by underlining that the region had been nuclearized long before the countries carried out their respective nuclear tests in May 1998.

The Islamabad correspondent of *The Hindu*, Amit Baruah, highlighted the lack of outcome, complaining that the talks had 'made little headway',[6] even as he acknowledged that it was futile to expect any sort of 'agreement' on an issue like Jammu and Kashmir in just two sessions of talks: 'Given the propaganda on both sides of the border (more so in Pakistan), the possibility of the two sides adopting a conciliatory approach also appears remote.'

The joint statement issued at the conclusion of the talks was unsurprisingly bland. It was a clear giveaway that the talks had not really helped progress on the issues under discussion.[7] The other six issues to be discussed as part of the Composite Dialogue,

---

[6] Amit Baruah, 'Stifling straightjacket', *Frontline*, 7 November 1998.

[7] The meeting on 16 October 1998 discussed issues of peace and security, including confidence-building measures. Both sides underscored their commitment to reduce the risk of a conflict by building mutual confidence in the nuclear and conventional fields.

The meeting on 17 October discussed Jammu and Kashmir. **The two sides reiterated their respective positions** (emphasis added).

were discussed in the next round of talks that followed in New Delhi in November 1998. Prospects of bilateral trade and export of electricity to India were discussed there.

Though there was not much progress at the talks in Islamabad, the desire for peace remained strong on both sides. It was also considered an opportune time for improving relations between India and Pakistan. With the right of centre, the nationalist Bharatiya Janata Party (BJP) coming to power in March 1998 in India and the Muslim League in power in Pakistan, analysts felt that both the countries were in a good position to take hard decisions. The BJP was known in Islamabad as an anti-Pakistan political party. The Muslim League, too, was known for its anti-India views. Despite the political orientation of his political party, India's prime minister Vajpayee was regarded as a moderate leader. Pakistani prime minister Nawaz Sharif was also known for his interest in developing relations with India. As a businessman from Lahore, it was said that he understood the benefits of good relations with India better than anyone else. I remember talking to a taxi driver in Lahore along these lines.

The sense of hope was strengthened by Sharif's congratulatory message on the assumption of the Prime Minister's Office by Vajpayee and the latter's cordial response. The desire to break out of the past and build a new paradigm for India–Pakistan relations seemed strong. The time seemed right, with both countries led by popularly elected leaders representing right-of-centre ideologies.

In early February 1999, in an interview to Shekhar Gupta, the then editor of the *Indian Express*, Sharif invited Vajpayee to Pakistan, 'Start the bus, he said, and invited Vajpayee to be on it. He will ensure a welcome, he said, that history will remember.'[8]

---

[8] Shekhar Gupta, 'The real story behind Vajpayee's bus trip to Lahore', Rediff.com, 29 August 2018.

Before the interview, Sharif had reportedly told Gupta that he would be extending this invitation on the condition that he didn't lose face and wasn't rebuffed. Gupta had conveyed this to Vajpayee and had received a 'yes' to Sharif's invitation. On the morning that the interview was published, Vajpayee landed in his constituency, Lucknow. When the press asked about Sharif's invitation, he said, 'Yes, I would like to have a bus ride to Pakistan.'[9]

On 20 February 1999, Vajpayee set off in a 'gleaming deep-gold-coloured luxury coach, with the Indian and Pakistani flags and the name of the bus, Sada-e-Sarhad (Call of the Frontier), painted on its front . . .(and) drove towards the Radcliffe Line, that blood-drenched line drawn by retreating British imperialists in 1947 which separated the mortal enemies who had fought three wars',[10] to inaugurate the Delhi–Lahore bus service, at the invitation of Pakistan Prime Minister Nawaz Sharif. Twenty-five celebrities travelled with him on the bus, including actors Dev Anand and Shatrughan Sinha, cricketer Kapil Dev, sculptor Satish Gujral, lyricist Javed Akhtar, danseuse Mallika Sarabhai and the late Alkali Dal leader Prakash Singh Badal.

This was a historic moment. A prime minister from a so-called 'Hindu nationalist party', head of a government that had just tested nuclear weapons, was journeying towards his Muslim counterpart, the head of a government of an Islamic Republic, which had also recently tested the atomic bomb.[11]

Prime Minister Sharif was waiting on the red carpet, as Prime Minister Vajpayee stepped off the bus on the Pakistan side of the

---

[9] Excerpts of Sagarika Ghose's biography of Atal Bihari Vajpayee, published in Scroll.in titled 'When Vajpayee defied hardliners to visit Pakistan as prime minister with a call for friendship', 6 January 2022.

[10] Ibid.

[11] Ibid.

Wagah–Attari border. They embraced warmly and shook hands. A twenty-one-gun salute announced the warm welcome extended to the Indian prime minister.

I was standing with the media party covering the landmark border crossing by the Indian prime minister, barely a few yards behind Prime Minister Sharif. The uniqueness of the moment had created a virtual storm in the media world. An unprecedented number of journalists had made their way to Lahore to cover the historic Lahore summit.

Ahead of the visit, as per established practice, an advance team had arrived in Lahore. High media interest was expected. We had booked an entire hotel for the Indian media party. Even with the entire hotel at our disposal, the accommodation ran short, and a couple of the official media representatives had to share rooms. As the Officer on Special Duty (Press Relations) in the Ministry of External Affairs, my friend and batchmate, Sunil Lal, had come with the Indian media. He and his team spent the night working with their Pakistani counterparts to get the accreditation documents ready for the large Indian media party.

On arrival, Vajpayee described his visit as 'a defining moment in South Asian history' expressing the hope that 'we will be able to rise to the challenge'.[12] He conveyed the goodwill of the Indian people and their desire to live in abiding peace and harmony with Pakistan. Prime Minister Sharif expressed similar sentiments. As the two leaders greeted each other warmly, embracing and shaking hands, it seemed possible for both nations to put the history of acrimony behind them.

In keeping with diplomatic practice and courtesy, Prime Minister Vajpayee had brought with him thoughtful and

---

[12] Srijan Sharma and Sajid Ali, 'The bus ride that almost helped Vajpayee Sharif rewrite history of South Asia', ThePrint, 1 July 2019.

personalized gifts. Prime Minister Sharif had a well-known fondness for old Bollywood movies; he was presented with CDs of Hindi film classics such as *Pakeezah* and *Mughal-e-Azam*, while beautiful shawls were brought for Begum Kulsoom Nawaz Sharif.

Vajpayee had a full programme for the visit. With a banquet hosted by Sharif in honour of the Indian prime minister and his delegation at Lahore Fort, on the same evening, the programme included visits to Minar-e-Pakistan, Mausoleum of Allama Muhammad Iqbal, Gurdwara Dera Sahib and Samadhi of Maharaja Ranjit Singh, in addition to the official talks. A civic reception in his honour at the Governor's House on 21 February introduced him to the gentry of Lahore.

The official banquet in the magnificent Diwan-i-Khas at Lahore Fort was a grand event. It was said that Prime Minister Sharif had personally supervised the arrangements. Twinkling lights glittered all around in the darkness of the night, creating a festive mood. Soft melodious music wafted through the air. I suddenly came alive to the music when it started playing the romantic Bollywood song, '*Baharon phool barsao, Mera mehboob aaya hai, Hawaon ragini gao, Mera mehboob aaya hai.*'[13] The dinner spread was lavish by any standards. Both leaders seemed inspired. The tone was set by Vajpayee's quote of a verse of the eleventh-century poet Mas'ud bin S'ad bin Salman, and Sharif's quote from Vajpayee's poem '*Jung na hone denge . . .*' (We will not allow war . . .).

The sense of peace, harmony and friendship did not extend to every section of the Pakistani society. The hard-line Jamaat-e-Islami was making threatening sounds. Due to the security challenges, Vajpayee had travelled from the Wagah border to Lahore by helicopter.

---

[13] Translated as: O fragrant bowers, make a shower of flowers, For my beloved has come; Blow gently O breeze, and sing through the trees, For my beloved has come.

There was a sense of disquiet within the Indian delegation. On 20 February 1999, terrorists killed twenty Hindu villagers, including six women, one girl and several members of a marriage party, in three villages in the Udhampur and Rajouri districts of Jammu. The army claimed that the Pakistan-based LeT was responsible for the killings.[14] According to General V.P. Malik, the then India's Chief of Army Staff (COAS), Indian military intelligence also intercepted several radio messages from across the border exhorting all jehadi elements inside Jammu and Kashmir to increase the level of violence. There was a sudden spurt in the elements' activities in Jammu and Kashmir. On 20 February, terrorists killed seven Hindu civilians at a wedding party at Bela Tilala in the Rajouri district. Four more were shot dead at Mora Putta in the same district.[15]

In the evening, Prime Minister Vajpayee's carcade was prepared in the drive of the Governor's House in Lahore ahead of the dinner. As per practice, the younger and junior members of the delegation accompanying the prime minister were seated in the respective cars ahead of time. Though the carcade was all set, the time listed for departure passed without any movement; senior members of the delegation were yet to come out. The banquet was obviously going to be delayed!

As we wondered about the cause of the unusual tardiness, we heard that the situation outside was belligerent. The Jamaat-e-Islami had a strong presence in Lahore and was bitterly opposed to Vajpayee's visit. On 20 February, it organized a series of rallies in Lahore to protest the visit by the Indian prime minister. A report

---

[14] US Department of State Annual Report on International Religious Freedom for 1999: India; Released by the Bureau for Democracy, Human Rights, and Labour, Washington, DC, 9 September 1999.

[15] General V.P. Malik, *Kargil: From Surprise to Victory*, HarperCollins, a joint venture with *India Today*, p. 32.

in Pakistani monthly magazine, *Herald*,[16] said that while enforcing their anti-Vajpayee campaign, hundreds of Jamaat workers went on the rampage burning tyres, smashing windows of private and diplomatic vehicles, forcing shops to shut down, and killing a police constable in the process. Shopkeepers had hardly opened their shutters when Jamaat activists started patrolling the city in trucks and lorries, forcing traders to close shop and manhandling those who resisted. The police looked on silently. The party ended its 'Go Back Vajpayee' rally at around 6 p.m., after which its workers went on to block the road to the fort where the banquet was being held in honour of the visiting prime minister. While blocking the road to the fort, Jamaat workers attacked the vehicles of some legislators, ministers and foreign ambassadors who were on their way to the banquet. The city administration put an end to the demonstrations the following day when it cordoned off a Jamaat meeting in front of its office and arrested 1300 party workers.

I only learnt after dinner that there had been pitched battles between the police and Jamaat cadres not far from where we were sitting and having dinner. The area around the Governor's House, had been turned into a virtual fortress. Access was severely restricted and was only relaxed somewhat for the civic reception hosted on Sunday evening (21 February) in honour of Vajpayee. The city of Lahore was under a security vigil.

According to an account by Pakistani commentator, Amjad Abbas Maggsi, the Chinese defence minister was also scheduled to visit Pakistan on 20 February.[17] There was no flexibility in Vajpayee's programme as the budget session of the Indian

---

[16] A monthly political and current affairs magazine of Pakistan's Dawn Media Group from 1970 to 2019 published from Karachi that broke several news stories.

[17] Amjad Abbas Maggsi, 'Lahore Declaration February 1999: A Major Initiative for Peace in South Asia', *Pakistan Vision*, Vol. 14, No. 1.

Parliament was to start from 22 February. Maggsi claims that Pakistan's foreign minister, Sartaj Aziz, was scheduled to receive the Chinese minister along with three services chiefs at Islamabad airport on 20 February. They were to arrive thereafter at Lahore to join the formal reception line-up for the Indian prime minister at the Governor House, before returning to Islamabad in the evening to attend the banquet for the Chinese defence minister. As per this account, it had been decided in a meeting presided by Prime Minister Nawaz Sharif (also attended by Army Chief General Pervez Musharraf) that Foreign Minister Sartaj Aziz and three services chiefs would receive the Chinese guest at Islamabad while the prime minister would receive the Indian prime minister at Wagah, Lahore. Qazi Hussain Ahmad of the Jama'at-e-Islami speculated in the media on 21 February that the services chiefs had refused to receive the Indian prime minister.

The involvement of Pakistan's 'agencies' working against the peace process was widely suspected. In an interview to Pakistani daily *Dawn*, Nawaz Sharif said some years after he was deposed that he learnt later that the stone-pelting on the cars of diplomats and processions against Vajpayee's visit to Lahore in February 1999 were stage-managed and orchestrated by the 'agencies' through a politico-religious party.

Being a seasoned political leader, Vajpayee remained unfazed by these developments and was said to be charmed[18] despite the protests.

On 21 February, Vajpayee visited the Minar-e-Pakistan. This was the site where the All-India Muslim League had called for a separate homeland for the Muslims of British India on 23 March 1940 by passing the Lahore Resolution, later called the Pakistan

---

[18] Sagarika Ghose, 'When Vajpayee defied hardliners to visit Pakistan as prime minister with a call for friendship', book excerpt in Scroll.in

Resolution. A seventy-metre-tall tower was built at the site between 1960 and 1968.

In a strong statement, Vajpayee wrote in the visitor's book there, 'A strong, stable and prosperous Pakistan is in India's interest. Let no one in Pakistan be in doubt. India sincerely wishes Pakistan well.'[19]

This was truly unprecedented for a leader of a party that had always rejected Partition and stood for 'Akhand Bharat', a united and undivided India. It demonstrated enormous political courage for Vajpayee to have visited the monument built to commemorate a separate Muslim nationhood and the 'two-nation theory'.

A large civic reception was held at the Governor's House on the evening of 21 February, where Vajpayee delighted the audience with his well-known oratorial skills. His Hindi was easily understood by the Urdu-speaking elite of Lahore. The spontaneous response seemed to indicate that many in the crowd agreed with him, especially when he said that 'partition (of India) had hurt, but the wound had healed; only the scar remained', adding that while they had opposed 'Partition, what had happened was a reality, a fact of life'. He reiterated his belief that: 'We can change history but not geography. We can change friends but not neighbours. Let us start walking together.'[20]

Vajpayee made a powerful point about his visit to Minar-e-Pakistan, saying, 'When I go back home, some people in my party will say that by going to the Minar-e-Pakistan I have placed my mohar (seal) on Pakistan,' *Kya Pakistan meri mohar se chalta hai? Pakistan ki apni mohar hai, aur woh chal raha hai.*' (Does

[19] Sagarika Ghose, 'When Vajpayee defied hardliners to visit Pakistan as prime minister with a call for friendship', book excerpt in Scroll.in.

[20] Sharat Pradhan, 'Vajpayee promises to ease visa restrictions on Pakistanis', Rediff on the net, 21 February 1999; 'We can change history but not geography . . .' *Chicago Tribune*, by contributed content, 28 February 1999.

Pakistan need my seal of consent? Pakistan has its own seal, and it works.)[21] . . . Pakistan is a reality, we want it to grow and thrive . . . there has been so much enmity, let's give friendship an opportunity . . . In these 24 hours I feel the distance between Delhi and Lahore has become a little less . . .'

Vajpayee's Lahore visit made a deep impact. About a month later, I was going to Delhi from Islamabad on 'Courier Duty', carrying the diplomatic bag by hand. At the Lahore airport, I went to the large VIP lounge to wait for my connecting flight. To my surprise, I found people glued to the many TV sets in the lounge, all listening avidly to the telecast of Vajpayee's speech delivered at the Governor's house almost a month back.

It is for good reason that political analysts have compared Vajpayee's Lahore visit to that of US President Nixon's to China in 1972. The success of the visit lay in Vajpayee's clear message of India's desire to live in peace with Pakistan; that India stood ready to walk the talk. The visit had substantive outcomes: the Lahore Declaration signed by the two prime ministers on 21 February 1999, a memorandum of understanding signed by the foreign secretaries of both countries and a joint statement.

The Lahore Declaration of 1999 provided the framework for peaceful relations between India and Pakistan. It represented the commitment of both leaders to normalize relations, taking the two countries on the path of peace and prosperity, and making South Asia a peaceful region. Even as both leaders remained cognisant of the many challenges, Lahore Declaration was a positive step and represented a vision that seemed to be saying not just 'Let's be friends' but also 'Let's be normal'.[22]

---

[21] Sagarika Ghose, 'When Vajpayee defied hardliners to visit Pakistan as prime minister with a call for friendship', book excerpt in Scroll.in

[22] Brooke Unger, 'Not Cricket', The Economist, Special Report, A survey of India and Pakistan, 20 May 1999.

The visit seemed a turning point in the bitter history of India and Pakistan. At that moment, in February's mild wintery sunshine in Lahore, it seemed impossible to imagine that within less than three months, India and Pakistan would be at war.

10

LoC Heats Up Conflict in Kargil

By February 1999, we had spent over half of our tenure in Islamabad but had not been able to travel outside the capital as a family. In late April, we started planning a family outing to Swat valley in western Pakistan. Swat used to be a centre of Gandharan Buddhism under the ancient Gandhara kingdom. Located on the picturesque Swat River at a height of almost 1000 metres, the region's cooler temperatures beckoned many a visitor from the summer heat of Islamabad. The region's lush forests, verdant unspoilt meadows, and snow-peaked Himalayas drew in the tourists as much as its unique culture and history. In the beginning of May, I spoke to a hotel in Swat to check availability during the coming weeks.

As I put the phone down, I recalled newspaper reports of heavy firing along the Line of Control (LoC). It seemed advisable to wait before making any advance payment or applying for leave. I was unaware then that Pakistani soldiers had infiltrated into areas on the Indian side of the LoC; covertly setting up bases over 130 vantage points. Apparently, the infiltrators had come prepared to stay equipped with small arms, grenade launchers, mortars, artillery and anti-aircraft guns. Many posts were later found to be heavily mined and more than 8000 anti-personnel mines were subsequently discovered by the Indian Army. It was thought that the bulk of the infiltration occurred in April, though some vacant posts were occupied in February 1999 itself. The heavy artillery fire from the Pakistani side would distract the attention of the Indian soldiers and provide cover for covert movements.

Due to the high snow-peaked mountains and the bitterly cold winters, in keeping with established practice, Indian patrols were not sent into some of the areas that were infiltrated by the Pakistani forces. The incursions, thus, remained undetected initially. It was some local shepherds grazing their sheep in the upper reaches of the mountains in the Batalik sector, who accidentally spotted the intrusion and reported it to the Indian Army on 3 May. Even after the infiltration was exposed, there wasn't enough knowledge of its nature or extent. Initially, the Indian troops in the area assumed that the infiltrators were jihadis. It was only after the discovery of the infiltration elsewhere along the LoC and the tactics they used that the scale of the infiltration and the involvement of the Pakistan Army became apparent.

As the extent of the Pakistani intrusions were exposed, the audacity of the move became clearer: Intrusions were spread over lower Mushkoh Valley in Dras, as well as in Kargil, Batalik, Chorbut La and Turtuk sectors south of the Siachen area. Our military adviser in the Mission once underlined the virtual impossibility of the task faced by the Indian Army: in military circles occupation of heights is considered vital, he said. 'The force occupying the heights can kill those trying to climb up the mountain simply by throwing down rocks at them; they do not even need bullets,' he explained. In an article titled 'Kargil: How

Much "By the Throat" Did the Pakistan Army Have Us?' General Syed Ata Hasnain, clarified, 'Anyone who knows high altitude operations can assess that to dislodge a well-entrenched defender at these heights would need an advantage of 9:1.'[1]

Pakistani briefings initially described the infiltration as a 'limited probe', a line that some US-based analysts adopted based on these briefings.[2] A 'limited probe' would be a small-scale incursion to learn about occupied/unoccupied areas and to assess the adversary's capability to defend those areas. The ability to return to home ground, or reverse the course without conflict escalation, is said to be one of the main features of a limited probe. The risk involved is, thus, limited and controllable. Intrusions in Kargil were far too extensive to be described as a 'limited probe'. Pakistani troops had intruded 8–10 kilometres into the Indian side of the LoC across a boundary of 160 kilometres! They were able to effectively interdict a vital communication link: the Srinagar–Kargil–Leh Highway. The entire civilian population of Ladakh and the military forces deployed there were dependent on this highway for most of their sustenance. It was assessed that Pakistan had infiltrated nearly one-and-a-half brigade-strength force into the strategically sensitive areas. Serious combat was inevitable.

Pakistani political and military objectives seemed strategic in nature. The concept, planning and preparation were said to have been worked out or confirmed at the Pakistan Army's general headquarters level. This included posting of additional officers to the Northern Light Infantry Regiment battalions, providing additional combat and logistical support and chalking out the radio deception plan.

---

[1] Syed Ata Hasnain, 'Kargil: How Much "By the Throat" Did the Pakistan Army Have Us?' *Swarajya*, 26 July 2019.

[2] General V.P. Malik, *Kargil: From Surprise to Victory*, p. 127.

Of immediate concern to India was the occupation of strategic locations overlooking National Highway 1 (NH1) connecting Srinagar with Leh (Ladakh) further north and the main supply route to the Indian forces in Siachen. With NH1 within range of Pakistani fire, the arterial logistic and supply route to Leh and Siachen was compromised. NH1 was a narrow road. The high altitude and rough mountainous terrain kept traffic slow. Pakistanis had a clear line of sight from their observation posts. They used this advantage to inflict heavy casualties by keeping artillery fire on sections of NH1. India's options were limited due to the high altitude.

The Indian armed forces started with efforts to recapture hills overlooking NH1, particularly stretches of the highway near the town of Kargil. By mid-May, additional soldiers were moved from the Kashmir valley to Kargil district. About 250 artillery guns were also brought in to support the soldiers attempting to recapture occupied peaks. The guns played a vital role.

In many places, however, there was not enough space or depth to deploy the guns. In other places, the outposts were out of visible range. In these locations, neither artillery nor air power could dislodge the occupied outposts. In such places, there was no option but to mount ground assaults on peaks that rose steeply to heights of 5500 metres. The attacks had to proceed at night, under the cover of darkness to avoid the prying eyes of intruders. Windy conditions and extremely low temperatures near the mountain tops added to the challenge. The assaults were slow and took their toll on the Indian forces. The heavy casualties and costly frontal attacks could have been avoided by blockading the Pakistani supply routes. This could only be done if the Indian troops crossed the LoC and carried out aerial attacks on Pakistani soil, risking expansion of the theatre of war. India chose to restrict the operations to a specific region instead of risking an all-out war with Pakistan. This made the job of the Indian Army extremely difficult.

General V.P. Malik, India's COAS during the Kargil War, writes in his book *Kargil: From Surprise to Victory*,

> On behalf of the COSC [Chairman Chiefs of Staff Committee], I then sought permission for the use of air power and the deployment of the Navy. The CCS [Cabinet Committee on Security] approved our proposal readily and wanted the intrusion along the LoC to be cleared at the earliest. EAM [External Affairs Minister] Jaswant Singh insisted that our forces should not cross the LoC or the international border. NSA [National Security Advisor] Brajesh Mishra, on behalf of the CCS, reiterated this statement as a term of reference.[3]

Such a 'restraint' at this juncture was understandable. Pakistan's political motives were not clear, neither was the identity of the intruders doubtful. There was no clarity on whether the Pakistan Army was using jehadi militants or carrying out the operation by itself. 'Besides, a war effort at the national level required a great deal of preparation. A considerable amount of work had to be done on the diplomatic front, particularly because only the previous year (1998) India and Pakistan had blasted their way out of nuclear ambiguity and had upset the United States of America and other powers, including the UK, China and Japan. The nuclear factor too must have been weighing on the mind of the prime minister and his CCS colleagues, though this aspect was never mentioned or discussed in the meetings.'[4] A significant feature of the Kargil War that will be remembered is the self-imposed national strategy of restraint that kept the war limited to the Kargil–Siachen sector.

---

[3] General V.P. Malik, *Kargil: From Surprise to Victory*, pp. 125–26.
[4] Ibid., p. 126.

Airstrikes by the Indian Air Force (IAF) against suspected positions of the infiltrators began in the third week of May. The purpose was to support land forces and the mandate was to use limited air power and remain on the Indian side of the LoC. These limitations posed their own challenges. Apart from the heights involved, the rarefied air and poor weather conditions challenged the air force. With enemy positions at elevations of between 4300 and 5500 metres (14,000 to 18,000 feet), the stark backdrop of rocks and snow made for uncommonly difficult visual target acquisition.[5] The weather too imposed limits on bomb loads that could be carried and airstrips that could be used.

Indian Navy soon began aggressive patrols in northern Arabian Sea, potentially threatening Pakistan's sea-based oil and trade supplies. Pakistan was then reportedly left with just six days of fuel (POL) to sustain itself if a full-fledged war broke out.[6] The Western Naval Command deployed INS Taragiri on barrier patrol just off Dwarka on 21 May 1999.[7] The navy also supplemented the Western Fleet with selected units from the Eastern Fleet. The bringing in of the navy at early stages of the conflict served to highlight Pakistan's vulnerabilities, thus, impacting the duration of the conflict.

At the Mission, we discussed patterns of Pakistan's imports, including oil imports. We heard that Delhi had begun an analysis of the type, extent and origin of Pakistani imports based on available data for planning interdiction of Pakistani oil tankers, should the situation so warrant. This information must have reached the Pakistan Navy, as it appeared to go into a red-alert

---

[5] Benjamin Lambeth, 'Airpower at 18,000: The Indian Air Force in the Kargil War', Carnegie Endowment for International Peace, 20 September 2012.

[6] This was revealed subsequently by former Pakistani prime minister Nawaz Sharif.

[7] General V.P. Malik, *Kargil: From Surprise to Victory*, p. 130.

mode and 'its warships began escorting the oil tankers as they moved out from the Gulf to Karachi'.[8]

Being in Pakistan, we felt isolated from home. Yet, we were intimately connected with what was happening.

On 14 May 1999, Lieutenant Saurabh Kalia (Captain posthumously) and five other soldiers[9] on a patrol in the Kaksar sector in Ladakh mountains were encircled by a platoon of Pakistani rangers and captured after they ran out of ammunition. They were subjected to torture during the three weeks of captivity as was clear from the mutilated bodies returned by the Pakistan Army to the Indian Army. It was clear that the injuries were inflicted before they were shot. There was an uproar in India at this breach of Geneva Conventions involving torture and killing of prisoners of war. India's EAM, Jaswant Singh, condemned this, saying such conduct is not simply a breach of established norms, or a violation of international agreements; it is a civilizational crime against all humanity; it is a reversion to barbaric medievalism.[10] He asked his Pakistani counterpart, Sartaj Aziz, to identify and punish the culprits.

Those days, I was the acting deputy chief of Mission; the former incumbent had proceeded on his next assignment and his successor was yet to join. It was during the high commissioner's visit to Delhi for consultations that I was summoned by the Pakistan Foreign Office, as acting high commissioner.

From a mid-level counsellor in the Mission, I suddenly found myself in the firing line. At the time of joining the High Commission in Islamabad, there were other officers between me

[8] General V.P. Malik, *Kargil: From Surprise to Victory*, p. 131.
[9] Arjun Ram, Bhanwar Lal Bagaria, Bhika Ram Moondh, Moola Ram Bidyasar and Naresh Singh of the 4th Jat Regiment, 'The forgotten story of Kargil's hero: Captain Saurabh Kalia', *Times of India*, 26 July 2016; Facebook – Indian Military Photos
[10] Quoted by General V.P. Malik, *Kargil: From Surprise to Victory*, p. 209.

and the High Commissioner. My job was somewhat simpler as the Head of Chancery, with additional responsibility for the Information and Culture Wing of the High Commission. Due to changes in personnel and delay in the arrival of the new deputy high commissioner, I was suddenly the acting deputy high commissioner during this crisis period.

Having covered similar meetings earlier, I reminded myself that I had been well groomed. I called High Commissioner G. Parthasarathy in Delhi to get his instructions before going to the Pakistan foreign office. Though I did not expect Pakistan to accept the violation of their obligations under the Geneva Conventions on treatment of captured soldiers, I was nonetheless shocked when the director general (South Asia) brazenly peddled the line that there was no independent international observer at the post-mortem of the Indian soldiers.

Around this time, I called my parents to follow up on their plans to visit us in Islamabad. Like others, my mother was concerned about the evolving situation. When I asked her about their visit to Islamabad, she simply said, 'Maybe it is better if all of you come to Delhi this year.' Neither my husband nor I could leave station, but we agreed to send the children to Delhi. There was another family proceeding to Delhi a week later, so we decided to send our children with them to their grandparents.

Even as we faced these brutal developments and their accounts in the local media day in, day out, our personal lives proceeded as before. At times, we were even pleasantly surprised by the kindness extended to us by the average Pakistani. Good experiences could be had at any turn in Islamabad even during war.

In Islamabad, every summer, some Pakistani textile companies would introduce light cotton fabrics for women. The colours and prints would be specially chosen for each summer. These 'Lawn suits' used to be hugely anticipated and were designed for the warm summers in Pakistan. I had bought fabric for my mother and two sisters in Delhi. As we packed the bags for the children, I was in two minds about sending these to Delhi.

A day before the children's flight to Delhi, I went to my tailor. Out of the blue, he asked me about the suits for my mother, 'What happened, Baaji (elder sister in Urdu), you were to bring suits for your Ammi (mother)? Summer will get over before you get them tailored!'

I explained to him that my parents were unable to come and that there wasn't enough time to get them made before the children's departure the next day. 'So what Baaji,' he exclaimed, 'it's for your Ammi! Just bring the material and I will get them prepared by tomorrow morning.' I couldn't quite believe him and asked, 'Ten suits?' He said he would stop all other work and get it done. The next day, I gave him an hour more and reached at 11 a.m. He was ready, 'I told you the suits would be ready at 10 a.m., and so they were,' he said. He did not even ask for any extra charges for the urgent work; I had to force him to take something for his workmen who had spent the entire night working. Whatever was happening at the LoC had no impact on his warmth and affection.

A couple of years later, after the terrorist attack on India's Parliament by Pakistan-based terrorists, our high commissioner's wife returned to India from Islamabad. She carried a gift for me from Masterji, my tailor in Islamabad. He had bought some fabric and made a salwar suit for me. The next day, I received a trunk call from Islamabad in my office. It was Masterji, who wanted to know if I had liked the suit. He generously told me to let him know if I wanted anything else that he could send for me. I was holding the sensitive position of director (Pakistan) in the Ministry of External Affairs. I wondered what the agencies listening to the conversation on either side made of this peculiar relationship between a tailor and his former client.

For a working woman, the household is never too far; it can beckon any time, be it war or peace! In the middle of my preoccupation with what was happening on the LoC, one afternoon, I got a panicky call from home that there was no water left in our water tank. I drove to the water tanker office for booking a tanker to fill up the empty water tank at home. As I reached the office, there was someone ahead and only one tanker in sight. I was worried that we may not be able to get water for quite some time. Given the heated situation on the LoC, one couldn't be sure if they would even deliver the tanker to us. I walked somewhat diffidently into the small office for allocating tankers. To my surprise, they seemed to be expecting me and promised to send the tanker right away. I asked about the person who had come in ahead of me, as there was just one tanker left. 'He said to send the first tanker to you; they'll wait for the next one,' the official in-charge said casually. Apparently, the other person recognized the number plate of my car as he lived in the same neighbourhood. He had just decided to be a good neighbour. 'If only this sentiment could enlighten decision-makers,' I thought to myself!

Given the deteriorating situation, Khan Saheb, our landlord, was getting worried about our safety. He drove over from Peshawar one evening. We sat in the garden as I was down with a virus. He was a patriotic Pakistani citizen, with his first son in the army, but was concerned for us due to the situation along the LoC. He inquired if we needed anything.

'We are fine, Khan Saheb,' I assured him. He then made an astounding suggestion: To ensure our safety, he wanted to post some of his gunmen at our gate to keep ill-intentioned people away. I wondered about the reaction of the Pakistani establishment to one of their citizen's efforts to secure diplomats from the 'enemy country'. It took joint effort, with my husband, to dissuade him from undertaking what would have surely brought trouble to his door.

Meanwhile, efforts by the Indian forces to recapture occupied posts along the LoC continued. It was becoming clear that the conflict would get prolonged, and there was risk of things going out of control anytime. We had to be prepared to move into the Chancery in such a situation. My husband and I were both included in the list of essential staff who would stay back in Islamabad, should evacuation of non-essential staff become necessary. I had this somewhat irrational fear that in case of an untoward development, our children would be orphaned; unlike children of other officers, neither parent could be with our children in those stressful days. This bothered me immensely. I also worried about how the children themselves were coping with this separation.

I was relieved to find that my sister, Prachi, and her husband, Abhay, were keeping them happy with plenty of activity and good food. Our sons, Anant and Aniket, developed a strong unbreakable bond with their cousins, Ishan and Chinmay, during this period. They played basketball and cricket together. While Abhay took them bowling, Prachi fed them copious amounts of shahi paneer and other favourites. My youngest sister, Gunjan, lived near my parents' home with her husband, Dinesh, and daughter, Mehul. They were always around for the children. When the adults were away, the children played pranks, calling friends on the phone pretending to be someone else. They always got caught when our younger son, Aniket, took the phone. With his strong American accent and broken Hindi, he was always a dead giveaway. The support of my parents and sisters, Prachi and Gunjan, helped in reassuring us that the children remained well cared for in our absence.

In Islamabad, we had to ensure that our Chancery campus had sufficient supplies of everything—food, water, diesel for the generator and so on. Meticulous plans were made to prepare the Mission for any eventuality. A more important job was to leave nothing of value for intruders in case of a forced enemy break-in. Keeping only the essential files, all other significant material was moved to Delhi by hand. In any such situation, the drill is to keep only as much as can be destroyed within the time taken by an intruding force to reach sensitive material from the time of break-in. We worked extra hours, including the weekends, to ensure that only the most essential material remained in the building.

At home, Ghanashyam and I packed a bag each of essentials and kept them near the door so that in case of an emergency, we could move immediately. The two bags stayed ready next to the door throughout the crisis.

With the beginning of air operations against the occupied peaks by the IAF, the situation seemed to have taken a more serious turn. Sitting in Islamabad, it seemed logical to be prepared for the worst. Fortunately, the security staff lived in the Chancery building itself as did some others. There was a full-fledged kitchen and dining room for the staff on campus. In an emergency, the few remaining officers could easily stay there for days and weeks, if required. Though, the air operations were limited to the occupied peaks, I frequently had the irrational thought of how tragic it would be if the operations expanded, and we were killed by a bomb dropped by our own IAF. Fortunately, the conflict never went beyond the limited area. Though we were fully prepared, we never had to move to the Chancery building.

It was on 27 May that the IAF lost two aircraft. Group Captain K. Nachiketa piloting a MiG-27 strike aircraft on a mission, suffered engine failure, but ejected successfully. Squadron Leader Ajay Ahuja's aircraft was hit by a surface-to-air missile while trying to locate the lost aircraft and help the rescue attempts. We heard with dismay that though Ahuja had bailed out of his stricken plane and parachuted safely, he was killed by his captors. Reports in the Indian media that Ahuja was alive upon landing and was killed subsequently by Pakistani troops after capture, sparked a major uproar within India.[11] Angry public demonstrations broke out at his cremation, and near the Pakistani Mission in Delhi. Expectedly, Pakistan rejected these claims. Ajay Ahuja was posthumously awarded one of India's highest gallantry awards, the Vir Chakra.

Flight Lieutenant Nachiketa was captured by a Pakistan Army patrol after about three hours. Nachiketa fired his service pistol till he ran out of bullets and was arrested. He was taken to a prison in Rawalpindi, where he was beaten up by Pakistani soldiers until a senior officer intervened. He remained in the custody of Pakistani forces until he was handed over to the International Committee of the Red Cross (ICRC) which, in turn, handed him over to the Indian High Commissioner G. Parthasarathy, inside the premises of the High Commission.

The dignified transfer of Flt Lt Nachiketa was not what Pakistani authorities had intended. It was supposed to have been a public relations coup[12] for them. Once Nawaz Sharif announced that Flt Lt Nachiketa would be released, the information minister conveyed the time of the 'handing-over ceremony' at the Pakistan Foreign Office. Close to 100 foreign and local media personnel, collected inside the Foreign Office for the 'handing over'.

Being a former armed forces officer, Parthasarathy made it clear to the Pakistani Foreign Office that he would not allow the handing over to be turned into a spectacle, nor would India agree to lowering the dignity of an IAF officer. He refused to take over the custody of Flt Lt Nachiketa in the full glare of the media.

---

[11] *Times of India*, 'Pakistan has poor track record with captured soldiers', 28 February 2019, called it 'cold blooded murder' in this report twenty years later, saying 'Pakistan later returned Ahuja's body, but it bore point-blank bullet wounds, indicating he was captured and then shot dead'.

[12] Amit Baruah, 'When freedom was granted to captured pilot K. Nachiketa', *The Hindu*, 3 June 1999.

Inside the mission, we saw a deeply upset Parthasarathy, fuming with concern for the dignity of an officer of the Indian armed forces. Since the Pakistani prime minister had already announced the release that evening, its Foreign Office got in touch with the ICRC as the next best option. The ICRC delegates did not allow any question–answer session with the press during the 'handing over' at the Pakistan Foreign Office and Nachiketa reached his people in a dignified manner.

Throughout this time, Pakistan had been peddling the myth that its government had no links with the intruders in Kargil and that they were 'mujahideen'. This myth started unravelling as India began recapturing occupied peaks and official army identification documents, pay books, letters, personal diaries, etc., were discovered on dead Pakistani soldiers. Some of these were exposed and highlighted Pakistan's involvement in the conflict. One of these was the diary of a Pakistan Army Captain, Hussain Ahmad, of 12 Northern Light Infantry, whose patrol entered the Kargil sector in February 1999.[13] Pervez Musharraf visited this officer's patrol base on 28 March 1999, five weeks after the signing of the Lahore Declaration, and gave Rs 8000 'for sweets' to be distributed among 12 Northern Light Infantry personnel.

There were several reports in sections of the Pakistani media about discontent within families of Northern Light Infantry soldiers who had participated in the war but had got no credit or had died inside the Indian territory. The Pakistan Army had declined to accept their bodies after the war. General V.P. Malik

---

[13] Cited by several accounts: Sandeep Unnithan, 'Letters from Kargil', *India Today*, 15 July 2019; B.G. Verghese, 'Musharraf Drops Siachen/Kargil Bombshell, 24 October 2006, bgverghese.com; President Musharraf's book "Line of Fire" comes under fire for assorted lies and half-truths', *Deccan Herald*, 24 October 2006.

writes about a request received by him through the Indian defence attaché in London, soon after the war was over, for return of the body of a young Pakistani officer. The request was made by the London-based grandfather of Captain Taimur Malik, of Pakistan's Special Service Group, attached to 3 Northern Light Infantry, who had been killed at Point 5770. On receipt of this message, the Indian Army got the bodies of Taimur and others exhumed from the area and returned them to the Pakistan Army near Kargil, with proper military honours.[14]

Proof of the involvement of the highest level of Pakistan Army became available on 11 June, when India released intercepts of conversations between Pakistan's COAS General Pervez Musharraf and Chief of General Staff, Lt General Aziz Khan, during the former's visit to Beijing at the peak of the conflict. Aziz was reporting about a meeting chaired by Prime Minister Sharif with the service chiefs of Pakistan Air Force and Navy, and ground developments about the ongoing conflict. In response to a fear expressed of the danger of escalation to a war, the response given was that there was no such fear as the 'scruff (tooti) of their (militants) neck is in our hands, whenever you want, we could regulate it'.[15] This intercepted conversation was released to the public and distributed at a press conference in New Delhi as evidence of deliberate violation of the LoC by the Pakistan Army.

Another Pakistani lie that got nailed was that there was no clarity about the LoC. Pakistan had been claiming that the LoC was not clearly defined and was open to interpretation. Led by our high commissioner, we launched a briefing campaign for Islamabad-based diplomats to discredit this Pakistani claim. In India, the government completely busted this false claim: Army

---

[14] General V.P. Malik, *Kargil: From Surprise* to Victory, p. 208.

[15] General V.P. Malik's book *Kargil: From Surprise to Victory*, Appendix 2, Records of Telephone Conversations, The First Conversation186.

commanders of India and Pakistan had met in 1972 in Shimla, after the 1971 India–Pakistan War, to not just draw a line but also demarcate the LoC very minutely by specifying the grid line of every mountain peak. Signed grid maps of the LoC were shown at a press conference in Delhi to demolish Pakistan's excuses. General V.P. Malik clarified:

> Given the availability of precisely marked maps in both countries and of the global positioning system (GPS) capable of giving the exact location of any spot within 10 metres, it was not difficult to demolish the Pakistani disinformation campaign. We showed marked delineated maps signed by commanders from both sides to the media. And when a Survey of Pakistan map was captured at Tololing in June 1999, we were able to show the LoC markings on the Pakistan map also.[16]

As Indian diplomats in Islamabad, we had to keep track of the Pakistani media. I had held charge of the media desk in the Mission, but all officers were going through newspaper and TV reports. The media reports in Pakistan projected a false sense of Pakistani superiority and success. The Urdu media tended to be particularly one-sided and often offensive. Being far away from our home country, in the middle of war, reading enemy propaganda every day must have weighed on everyone, but it is to the credit of the entire team that the tenor of our internal meetings was always cheerful and upbeat. We almost always found something to laugh about.

By mid-June, it was clear that the tide was turning against Pakistan. Pressure from the international community was mounting as Pakistan's role in the incursions was becoming

---

[16] General V.P. Malik, *Kargil: From Surprise to Victory*, p. 66.

clearer with each revelation. Pressure was building up on Pakistan to withdraw its forces and use its influence over the so-called 'mujahideen' to vacate their infiltration.

Indian troops began recapturing strategic peaks. Pakistani presence on Tiger Hills, overlooking NH1 was a crucial bottleneck for the movement of both troops and supplies. Attempts to regain Tiger Hill in late May 1999 had remained unsuccessful. A fresh attempt began with artillery bombardment, as three Indian regiments (Sikh, Grenadiers and Naga) advanced up the left and right flanks of the mountain, while another, including a Ghatak[17] platoon, scaled a 1000-feet vertical cliff on the rear side of the mountain. The peak was captured after bitter fighting and considerable loss of life. Indian troops then secured Tololing in the Dras sector following fierce battle.

By the end of June, Pakistan began retreating. After an emergency meeting with Clinton sought by Pakistan, Prime Minister Sharif officially announced the Pakistan Army's withdrawal from Kargil. Indian forces continued their operations to take control of strategic peaks in Dras and Batalik. Indian prime minister Atal Bihari Vajpayee declared Operation Vijay a success on 14 July. The Kargil War officially ended on 26 July as the Indian Army announced the complete withdrawal of Pakistani irregular and regular forces. This day is observed as Kargil Vijay Diwas (Victory Day) in India.

---

[17] Ghatak Platoons or Ghatak Commandos are specially trained and selected troops that are part of all infantry battalions, which act as force multipliers and spearhead special tasks of the battalion. The name Ghatak was given by General Bipin Chandra Joshi. Their operational role could include carrying out tasks such as special reconnaissance, raids on enemy artillery positions, airfields, supply dumps and tactical headquarters or other special operations at a tactical level. (Maj. Gen. L.B. Chand (Retd), 'Indian Infantry's Ghatak Platoons: Ultimate, Invincible, Swift, Steadfast & Courageous', Aviation and Defence Universe).

As India celebrated a victory won after bitter sacrifices, the blame game started in Pakistan. Given that Kargil intrusions were discovered within two months of the historic Lahore visit, it was natural to wonder about Prime Minister Sharif's involvement in the decision-making. Some analysts were convinced that the blueprint of the attack was reactivated soon after Musharraf was appointed chief of army staff in October 1998. Sharif claimed that he was unaware of the plans; that he had learned about the situation only when he received an urgent phone call from Vajpayee. Sharif attributed the plan to Musharraf and 'just two or three of his cronies'.[18] This view was shared by some Pakistani writers as well, who stated that only three or four generals, including Musharraf, knew of the plan.[19] The assertion from Musharraf's side was that Sharif had been briefed on the Kargil operation fifteen days ahead of Vajpayee's journey to Lahore.

Following the Lahore visit, starting early March 1999, the prime ministers of India and Pakistan had started secret Track-2 parleys through the back channel, using Indian political journalist R.K. Mishra, and a Pakistani diplomat Niaz Naik, in New Delhi and Islamabad. On 12 and 21 April, Vajpayee reportedly conveyed (through Mishra) to his counterpart, Sharif, that there was no let-up in the infiltration of militants from Pakistan, and Sharif replied that he 'would use his influence to correct the situation'.[20]

The late Pakistani prime minister Benazir Bhutto revealed in an interview to Shyam Bhatia, senior editor of *India Abroad*, that

---

[18] PTI, 'Nawaz blames Musharraf for Kargil', *Times of India*, 28 May 2006.

[19] PTI, 'Musharraf behind Kargil war: Nawaz Sharif', 21 February 2009, provides an illustration of this line of argument.

[20] General V.P. Malik, *Kargil: From Surprise to Victory*, p. 33, quoting from Robert G. Wirsing, *Kashmir: In the Shadow of War Regional Rivalries in a Nuclear Age* (M.E. Sharpe, New York, p. 29).

Musharraf had harboured ambitions of capturing Srinagar long before the Kargil war.[21] Musharraf, as her director general (Military Operations), had outlined a plan to infiltrate Mujahideen into Kashmir with the objective of capturing Srinagar, which she had dismissed due to the lack of clarity about the next steps.

It appears likely that senior Pakistan Army officers did not fully explain details of the Kargil operation to Sharif. But there are also suggestions that Sharif may have known before the Lahore Declaration could be signed that a Pakistan Army-controlled offensive action across the LoC was being undertaken in Kargil.

Apparently, Musharraf's plan had hinged on the assumption that India would be forced to open a second front after failure to dislodge the well-entrenched 'mujahideen' from their positions and a worried international community would pressurize India to back off, leaving Srinagar in Pakistan's grasp. As it turned out, India did not play the game along Pakistani assumptions. Indian forces were able to drive out the 'mujahideen' and Pakistani forces from their well-entrenched positions. India recaptured occupied areas, without getting into Pakistani territory and without opening a second front. This, coupled with India's strong and sustained diplomatic campaign, pushed Pakistan on the back foot. Reports of shortages in the Pakistani trenches, be it food or bullets, found their way into the media, including stories that appeared later claiming that Pakistani soldiers were found with grass in their stomachs![22]

---

[21] 'The Benazir interview Pakistan finds treasonous!' Rediff.com, 4 September 2003.

[22] Tilak Devasher, 'Tilak Devasher writes on Pervez Musharraf: How Kargil War, his pet project, ended up drawing US and India closer', *Indian Express*, 6 February 2023, https://indianexpress.com/article/opinion/columns/tilak-devasher-pervez-musharraf-kargil-war-us-india-8426618/.

The Pakistan Army's plan was obviously poorly conceived, extremely naive, completely misjudging of India's capability and resolve and, thus, not clearly thought through.

Musharraf later described Kargil as a 'landmark' in Pakistan Army's history in military terms, given that 'just five Pakistani battalions' in support of the 'freedom fighter groups' could compel the deployment of more than four Indian divisions.[23] While being a severe exaggeration, this amounted to an official confirmation by the Pakistan government of the heavy involvement of its military in Kargil. This could be seen as the emergence of a new warfare technique. A.K. Doval, National Security Advisor to Prime Minister Narendra Modi, interpreted it as an admission 'that Islamic militants are an integral part of Pakistani army and are working in tandem'. He saw this as having become 'a war machine' requiring India to modify its techniques accordingly.[24]

There can be discussion over who was responsible for planning of Kargil or how much Sharif knew about it or when he learnt of what was going on. One thing, however, is indisputable: The Kargil War managed to kill the trust and bonhomie created just a few months back by Vajpayee's landmark crossing of the border at Lahore.

---

[23] General V.P. Malik, then Indian COAS, *Kargil: From Surprise to Victory* (online version): the troop enhancement was nowhere near the claims made by General Musharraf (in his book): 'India had only 3 Infantry Division east of the Zoji La pass before the war. Also, 8 Mountain Division was inducted in end May 1999. Only these two divisions fought the war in Kargil. Yes! We had additional forces poised at different locations elsewhere for crossing the LoC or the international border - some at very short notice - should the need arise'.

[24] Raj Chengappa and Sandeep Unnithan, 'From the archives (2006); Pervez Musharraf's memoirs: Myths vs reality', *India Today*, 14 June 2022.

The debate over the Kargil debacle raged on relentlessly in Pakistan over the coming months, until it was obvious that something would have to 'give'!

11

Military Coup: Someone Has to Take the Rap

In the second half of 1999, Pakistan's economy was in dire straits and international opinion not very sympathetic. Intrusions in Kargil were an unacceptable and unnecessary betrayal after Prime Minister Vajpayee's Lahore visit and were seen as such by the wider international community. Facing defeat, Pakistan had to look for a face saver in Kargil.

The writing was on the wall, when Prime Minister Sharif made a rushed visit to the US to meet President Clinton in July 1999. President Clinton's special assistant for the near eastern and South Asian affairs at the national security council, Bruce O. Riedel was quoted some years later as saying that: '(Mr) Sharif . . . was bringing his wife and children with him to Washington, a possible indication that he was afraid he might not be able to go home if the summit failed or that the military was telling him to leave. At a minimum, (Mr) Sharif seemed to be hedging his bet on whether this would be a round trip.'[1]

After the Kargil War, India set up the Kargil Review Committee (KRC) to look at the overwhelming evidence that the Pakistani armed intrusion in the Kargil sector had come as a complete surprise to the Indian government, the army, intelligence agencies, as well as the Jammu and Kashmir government and its agencies. This led to an examination of the failures and measures required to prevent a repeat of a Kargil-like situation in future.

In Pakistan, a shadowy to and fro started. Stories emanating from the Sharif camp focused on laying the blame for the debacle entirely on Musharraf and 'his cronies' who had 'hatched the plans for the ill-conceived venture'; that it was Musharraf who pushed Nawaz Sharif to get the US involved in ending the Kargil conflict; that the dire straits of Pakistan's economy made it virtually impossible for Pakistan to have continued fighting the war; sections of the press also referred to shortages in the trenches in Kargil, including food and shells for soldiers.

Sections of the Pakistani media which had informal links with Pakistani armed forces peddled the false notion that the political leadership under Prime Minister Nawaz Sharif had lost a battle that had been won by the Pakistani military. This line of reporting tended to claim that Pakistan's political leadership lacked courage and had surrendered, thereby squandering the 'hard-earned victory' on the battlefield. Pakistani withdrawal from Kargil was projected as the country's capitulation to US pressure, humiliation of the Pakistan Army and forfeiture of a 'rare military victory' over India.

Refuting this myth, Raj Chengappa quotes the then COAS General V.P. Malik: 'When Sharif visited Washington, he saw

---

[1] Anwar Iqbal, 'Clinton adviser: confusion gripped Islamabad during Kargil crisis', *Dawn*, 23 October 2006.

the writing on the wall—we had already recaptured 90 percent of the occupied territory and most of the important heights including Tiger Hill.'[2] General Anthony Zinni, the then chief of the US Central Command, who visited Pakistan during that period, says in his book *Battle Ready*, 'The problem with the Pakistan leadership was the apparent national loss of face . . . what we (the US) were able to offer was a meeting with President Clinton . . . but would announce it only after the withdrawal of forces. That got Musharraf's attention and he encouraged Prime Minister Sharif to hear me out.'[3] Nawaz Sharif also claimed that, 'Mr. Musharraf felt we should bring Mr Clinton into the matter so that there would be an honourable end to Kargil. He pushed me to meet him.'[4]

The media in Pakistan wrote about the prevailing corruption and incompetence under the Sharif government. There were reports in the press that over 5000 large and medium industrial units were sick. Other reports indicated that announcements of schemes like construction of 5,00,000 houses for the poor or building of 5000 km of motorways connecting villages had failed to ignite the economy. It seemed that nothing could change the narrative; the announcements were seen as populist measures by a desperate leader. Under IMF pressure, Sharif was also forced to announce an unpopular hike of 15 per cent in sales tax on several food items and fuel. The uncontrolled sectarian violence and regular killing of Shia and Sunni Muslims in Pakistan added to his unpopularity.

---

[2] Raj Chengappa and Sandeep Unnithan, 'From the archives (2006); Pervez Musharraf's memoirs: Myths vs reality', *India Today*, 14 June 2022.

[3] 'Zinni's book throws light on Kargil withdrawal', *Dawn*, 4 June 2004.

[4] Raj Chengappa, 'I seriously wanted Kargil War to come to an end, says former Pakistan PM Nawaz Sharif', *India Today*, 26 July 2004.

Sensing that the government was on a weak wicket, the Opposition started agitating and holding protest marches. A major rally was organized in Lahore by around twelve opposition parties in September with the slogan 'Go, Nawaz, Go'.

Halfway through his second tenure, the most powerful civilian head of government ever, who had stared down a COAS,[5] a prime minister who had won a handsome political victory at the hustings, suddenly appeared vulnerable. With his dwindling popularity, an Opposition clearly impatient to oust him and a powerful military on his back, Sharif was faced with the most serious challenge of his career thus far.

Around this time, we were invited for dinner by a former COAS to his house in the powerful Rawalpindi cantonment. Indian diplomats were not allowed into the cantonment areas, but such rules did not apply to the mighty and powerful erstwhile army chief. The driver of our official vehicle went to a tea shop nearby after dropping us off. Soldiers gathered at the popular tea stand were avidly discussing the removal of Prime Minister Sharif. Obviously, this was the talk in the powerful 'Pindi garrison'. Sharif's days seemed numbered.

Few days later, I met my British counterpart for lunch. We discussed the ongoing shadow boxing between the political and military leadership. His analysis was simple: Kargil was a major national disaster for Pakistan, and someone would have to take the rap for it; someone's head would have to roll.

By September, tension between the two sides seemed to have escalated to near breaking point. The anxiety of the political

---

[5] General Musharraf was appointed as army chief for three years in October 1998 after his predecessor, General Jehangir Karamat, resigned following differences with Sharif. General Karamat was compelled to resign after he suggested the setting up of a national security council that would give the army and technocrats greater say in the running of the administration.

leadership seemed transparent when Nawaz Sharif's brother, Shahbaz Sharif, was sent as the PM's envoy to Washington in mid-September. According to Reidel, he and Rick Inderfurth, assistant secretary of state for South Asian Affairs under President Clinton, met with Shahbaz Sharif for hours in the latter's suite at the Willard Hotel.[6] Apparently, Shahbaz Sharif only wanted to discuss what the US could do to help his brother stay in power: 'He all but said that they knew a military coup was coming.'

On 29 September, Prime Minister Sharif extended the tenure of General Musharraf as chairman of the Joint Chiefs of Staff Committee[7] (CJCSC). The naval chief, Admiral Fasih Bokhari, resigned on 2 October, seven months ahead of the end of his tenure. The extension of General Musharraf as CJCSC, was seen as a conciliatory move, obviously under duress. This was in sharp contrast to the confident prime minister who had stared down the former COAS, General Jehangir Karamat.

The suspense in the thrilling saga of politico-military tussle peaked in early October. The dam burst on 12 October 1999. It was Nawaz Sharif's own actions that precipitated the coup, giving the military a chance to call it a 'counter-coup'.

The dramatic events started unfolding a few hours after the official news service reported at about 5 p.m. on 12 October that General Musharraf was being immediately retired. At the Mission, officers collected around the TV in Parthasarathy's room and watched in fascination as Nawaz Sharif promoted Lt General Khawaja Ziauddin Abbasi, director of the ISI, to full general and made him the new COAS.

The timing and manner of replacing General Musharraf as well as the choice of General Ziauddin were curious. Ziauddin

---

[6] 'Anwar Iqbal, 'Clinton adviser: Confusion gripped Islamabad during Kargil crisis', *Dawn*, 23 October 2006.

[7] The JCSC groups the army, air force and navy.

was the first army engineer and the first director of the ISI to be appointed to a four-star command appointment. He had spent his career in the military as an engineering officer of the Pakistan Army Corps of Engineers before taking over the ISI in October 1998. It is inconceivable that the politically savvy Sharif family did not realize that an officer from the non-fighting arm of the military was unlikely to be acceptable to the army as COAS.

Nawaz Sharif tried to exile Musharraf when the latter was on an official visit to Sri Lanka. In a dramatic move, Musharraf was dismissed when he was on a plane returning from Colombo. The announcement on Pakistan Television did not give any reason. Later, General Musharraf said in his speech that as he tried to return to Pakistan from Sri Lanka, his commercial flight, short of fuel, was ordered to land outside of Pakistan, endangering the lives of all the passengers.

A *New York Times* report by Tim Weiner colourfully describes the situation in Pakistan: 'For months, Pakistan's Prime Minister and its top general were like two scorpions in a bottle. This week, both struck.'[8]

The plane carrying General Musharraf was denied permission to land at Karachi International Airport by air traffic controllers. It circled for more than an hour, it circled, as its fuel ran low, and its pilot feared disaster. It landed with only minutes of fuel to spare. Within hours of landing in Karachi, General Musharraf was in control of Pakistan.

The entire episode ran like a suspense thriller. The Pakistan International Airlines (PIA) flight was ordered to be diverted to anywhere outside Pakistan, first Oman followed by India. On being told that the plane had insufficient fuel, the pilot was asked

---

8   Tim Weiner, 'Countdown to Pakistan's Coup: A Duel of Nerves in the Air', *New York Times*, 17 October 1999.

to go to Nawabshah, a small regional airport outside Karachi, after his unsuccessful attempts with the air traffic controls at Lahore and Islamabad airports. The pilot claimed later that he wasn't allowed to land at Nawabshah either. Another version claimed that the runway wasn't long enough for the aircraft to land. The lights at Karachi airport were switched off and the runway was blocked to prevent the flight from landing. According to the army, a police escort and a light plane dispatched by Prime Minister Sharif were waiting for General Musharraf at Nawabshah to arrest him and transport him to Islamabad.

As per the version of events given by the army, General Musharraf went to the cockpit and contacted the army's corps commander in Karachi, Lt General Muzaffar Usmani, for help by placing a call through Dubai with the help of the pilot. General Usmani and a commando team rushed to the Karachi Airport and seized control of the tower. The army chief was received at the airport by a large contingent of soldiers and left the airport accompanied by several Jeeps filled with soldiers.

Troops climbed over the fence of state-run Pakistan TV (PTV) and seized the PTV station in Islamabad. They surrounded the prime minister's marble residence, took over the international airports, cancelled all flights and cut the international phone lines. They also began moving through Islamabad, seizing the cabinet building and taking over homes of several Sharif ministers, including Information Minister Mushahid Hussain, Foreign Minister Sartaj Aziz, the Kashmir Affairs Minister Majid Malik and Accountability Chief Saif-ur Rehman, and putting them under house arrest. Nawaz Sharif, his brother Shahbaz, the chief minister of Punjab Province and the former ISI chief General Ziauddin were all taken into 'protective custody'. Eventually, Nawaz Sharif and his family were exiled to Saudi Arabia in 2000.

The TV came back on air sometime after the army had taken over control. Nawaz Sharif's government fell in a military coup, without a shot being fired.

As the coup was underway, there was confusion about exactly what was going on. The Spanish Embassy was hosting their national day reception that evening which we were deputed to attend. We drove past the Pakistan TV campus which was in complete darkness. At the Spanish reception, rumours were flying thick and fast about what was afoot. It was apparent that a military coup was underway, but details were a matter of speculation. At the end of the reception, we returned to the Mission. While sharing inputs we had gathered at the Spanish Reception with Delhi on phone, I realized that we were competing with 24/7 international news channels, who were reporting developments from different points in the city.

It was around 10.15 p.m. that the first official confirmation about the action taken by the army against the government came. A PTV newsreader announced that Nawaz Sharif had been dismissed. After midnight, the state television announced that all banks would be closed during the day.

Finally, around 3 a.m., General Musharraf appeared on TV and laid out the reasons for the coup: The country was in a state of 'turmoil and uncertainty', the economy in a state of collapse and systematic destruction of Pakistan's institutions. He claimed that the armed forces had taken over as a last resort to restore stability. 'I have done so with all sincerity, loyalty and selfless devotion to the country, with the armed forces firmly behind me,' he proclaimed.[9]

Not unexpectedly, the Clinton Administration appeared unhappy with the developments. A State Department spokesman

---

[9] 'The coup leader explains his motives for seizing power', Guardian, 12 October 1999.

said that if a coup were confirmed, the US would call for the earliest possible restoration of democracy and would not carry on 'business as usual' with Pakistan.[10] A senior Clinton Administration official referred to a similar message having been sent to the Pakistan Army through diplomatic channels earlier.

Clinton visited Pakistan at the end of a week-long visit to Bangladesh, India and Pakistan between 20 and 25 March 2000. Due to the military coup, there was considerable debate within the US establishment on whether Pakistan should be part of the trip to India. A report in the *New York Times*[11] cited a State Department official as describing the tussle over the visit as a 'fight to the finish' between security and anti-terrorist officials, who did not want Clinton to go, and those who believed it was essential not to write off Pakistan. While announcing the trip that was to start in Bangladesh, the White House stressed that the focus of Clinton's trip would be on India where he would spend five days and visit five cities. The itinerary in India was 'geared to spectacular backdrops—the Taj Mahal and possibly an elephant ride—and to emphasising the new India of technology and trade'. In contrast, said the report, Clinton may not venture outside the Islamabad airport, and stay only a few hours. 'Five days in India vs five hours in Pakistan' was a colourful phrase that a friend used to describe the contrast.

In view of the security concerns, President Clinton arrived in Pakistan under extraordinary security for his short visit. He came in an unmarked plane that landed after a decoy jet with official markings had touched down first. A Secret Service agent bearing

---

[10] Celia W. Dugger, 'Coup in Pakistan: The Overview; Pakistan Army Seizes Power Hours after Prime Minister Dismisses His Military Chief', *New York Times*, 13 October 1999.

[11] Jane Perlez, 'Clinton Decides to Visit Pakistan, After All', *New York Times*, 8 March 2000.

a resemblance to Clinton disembarked from the decoy plane. We were glued to the TV sets in the office, as first the decoy and then the US President's plane landed. Clinton was whisked off to meet General Musharraf, through roads cleared of people and heavily guarded by Pakistani soldiers.

After talks lasting two hours, Clinton spoke live on television for fifteen minutes. In his message to Pakistan, Clinton urged the government to restore democracy, reduce its nuclear arsenal, fight terrorism and find a peaceful solution to the Kashmir crisis with India. In his TV address, he told the Pakistanis that the US wanted to be a friend but cautioned that Pakistan's prolonged antagonism with India was draining the resources so needed to improve schools, public health and the economy.[12]

General Musharraf came on TV after Clinton's departure, wearing a white sherwani. The pressure of the US President's visit became obvious as he first wiped his profusely sweating forehead on live TV in the rather balmy Islamabad weather in March!

Nawaz Sharif's sudden action of sacking General Musharraf in October 1999 remains unexplained. It was clearly a risky proposition given that the military had ruled Pakistan for almost half of its fifty-two years as an independent nation (in 1999). Riskier perhaps, as Sharif had already replaced the former army chief a year earlier. What happened in the few days that followed the reappointment of General Musharraf as CJCSC that inspired Sharif's decision to fire General Musharraf? Perhaps, the extension as CJCSC was aimed at lulling the general's suspicions, or an olive branch to appease the increasingly powerful Musharraf.

The army has been the real ruler of Pakistan directly or indirectly behind the cover of a civilian government, ever since

---

[12] Charles Babington and Pamela Constable, 'Clinton, Aided by Decoy, Urges Peace on Pakistan', *Washington Post*, 25 March 2000.

General Ayub Khan staged a military coup in 1958. Privilege accompanied power for Pakistan's military as its tentacles spread into almost every sector of the country's economy—industry, agriculture and services. Pakistan's military owns everything, from fertilizer and hosiery factories to bakeries, petrol pumps, banks, cement, milk dairies, stud farms and golf courses. The military ruthlessly milked Pakistan's economy, benefiting military personnel (particularly the senior officers) most of whom have since become millionaires and some even billionaires.[13] In 2007, Ayesha Siddiqa, a former researcher with Pakistan's naval forces, estimated[14] that the military's net private wealth could be as high as $20 billion, a 'rough figure', split between $10 billion in land and $10 billion in private military assets.[15] $10 billion was roughly four times the total foreign direct investment generated by Islamabad in 2007.

While the Pakistan Military owns and runs several commercial entities, it is real estate that is the jewel in the military's crown. General Ayub Khan started the practice of allotting large tracts of prime land to military officers. The phenomenon multiplied exponentially over the years. The army owns 12 per cent of the country's land, its holdings being mostly fertile soil in eastern Punjab. Two-thirds of that land is in the hands of senior current and former officials, mostly brigadiers, major generals and generals. The most senior 100 military officials are estimated to be worth over $3.5 billion.[16]

---

[13] Markandey Katju, 'The truth about the Pakistan military', *Week*, 26 August 2019.

[14] Ayesha Siddiqa, *Military Inc: Inside Pakistan's Military Economy*, Penguin Random House India, Gurugram, 2017.

[15] 'Pakistani army's "$20bn" business', Al Jazeera, 8 July 2008.

[16] Assorted sources based on Ayesha Siddiqa's book *Military Inc: Inside Pakistan's Military Economy*.

The army is the largest business conglomerate in Pakistan, with more than fifty big business entities across Pakistan, most of whom are the largest in the country. Many of these businesses are run in the name of charitable organizations which are 'dedicated to the nation' and directly operated by senior army generals.[17] The Fauji Foundation is one of the most diversified business conglomerates in Southeast Asia, with more than twenty-five companies (four wholly owned and twenty-one associated companies, as per their own website). Not only does it sell everything from biscuits to sanitary napkins, but there are also reports of its entry into gold mining in Balochistan,[18] where people have been agitating for years over the aggressive abuse of its abundant natural resources amid widespread violations of human rights. Pakistan's *Dawn* newspaper reported the details of the commercial entities run by the armed forces as per details provided in the Senate in response to a question by PPP's Senator Farhatullah Babar.[19] Defence Minister Khwaja Asif informed through a written reply to the house that there were nearly fifty 'projects, units and housing colonies' functioning in the country under the administrative control of Fauji Foundation, Shaheen

---

[17] Soumyadipta Banerjee, 'Pakistan is desperately poor. Its army is rich beyond belief. How come?' *DailyO*, 25 March 2019.

[18] The Pakistan Army's role in seizing Baloch gold mines? *South Asia Monitor*, 10 June 2020. Prime Minister Imran Khan's commitment to set up a commission to investigate how Pakistan ended up owing around $6 billion to a mining company, which discovered gold and copper in Balochistan, found no takers. Reason: the army's 'neck-deep' role in seizing control of the mines at the cost of Pakistan's economy.

[19] Amir Wasim, '50 Commercial entities being run by the armed forces', *Dawn,* 21 July 2016.

Foundation, Bahria Foundation, Army Welfare Trust (AWT) and Defence Housing Authorities (DHAs).[20]

The military was also involved in public-sector organizations like the National Logistics Cell, the Frontier Works Organization and the Special Communications Organization, all of which are controlled by the army. The Water and Power Development Authority was placed under military control in 1998, with over 35,000 personnel involved in its operations. The influence of the Ministry of Defence helped secure public-sector business contracts and financial and industrial inputs at highly subsidised rates. Profit making by retired military personnel extended to providing privatized security services to foreign contractors in security-sensitive regions such as the Federally Administered Tribal Areas and Khyber Pakhtunkhwa (FATA and KPK). Several senior service officers were also sent as ambassadors, governors, and nominated on other high-ranking bureaucratic posts in Pakistan.

The smooth and speedy army action following the dismissal of General Musharraf on 12 October 1999, made people wonder if the military coup had been in the works over the preceding weeks. Some media reports based on military sources stated that the joint chiefs of staff, headed by General Musharraf, and the regional corps commanders had met on 18, 21 and 23 September to discuss the army's modus operandi in case Prime Minister Sharif moved against the army. Pakistani military analysts with known closeness to the establishment were quoted as saying that the intentions and attitude of Sharif towards the army were well

---

[20] According to the details provided in the reply, eight DHAs, mostly created through ordinances, were established in major cities and were in Karachi, Lahore, Rawalpindi-Islamabad, Multan, Gujranwala, Bahawalpur, Peshawar and Quetta.

known. The army chief anticipated some such move and had put in place a 'contingency plan' for it.

The warning signs had been clear for months. Pakistani officials and politicians had been conveying their fears to relevant quarters about the likelihood of a coup for over a month. If diplomats of the most-watched country in Islamabad, who were followed physically by intelligence agents, could hear rumblings from the ground, others would have been hearing it like the sound of thunder!

There were no widespread protests following the coup. Once it became clear that the military had taken over after unseating the democratically elected government, the media reported 'spontaneous' show of public support.

It is said that 'politics is a soldier's curse'. The murder of democracy by military coups in Pakistan has been justified by Pakistani courts under the 'Doctrine of Necessity'.[21] Unlike in Pakistan, the army in India does not meddle in Indian politics. The Indian Army has proudly followed the tradition of keeping a distance from politics and political power. Following the military coup in Pakistan, we gently ribbed Brigadier Das, our military adviser, for having joined the 'wrong army'. True to his uniform, he remained unfazed and responded confidently, 'Musharraf has just mounted the tiger. Let us see how he survives hereafter. Dismounting a tiger is not known to be easy.' I was reminded of these words, when in December 2019, a Pakistani court sentenced Musharraf to death in absentia in a case of high treason.

---

[21] The Doctrine of Necessity has its roots in the writings of Henry de Bracton, a medieval jurist, who stated 'that which is otherwise not lawful is made lawful by necessity'. In the controversial case of *Federation of Pakistan v. Maulvi Tamizuddin Khan* (1955), the chief justice of Pakistan, Muhammad Munir, legally validated the extra-constitutional use of emergency powers by Governor General Ghulam Mohammad and referred to the aforementioned maxim of Bracton, thus implementing the Doctrine of Necessity.

Support by sections of the Pakistani population to the military coup by General Musharraf, reminded me of Akbar Allahabadi's couplet: '*Hum aah bhi karte hain to ho jate hain badnam; Wo qatl bhi karte hain to charcha nahin hota.*' (I suffer slander, when I merely sigh; they get away with murder, without mention of it nigh.)

I would remember this couplet many times in the future, as countries lectured India to not get agitated by terrorism originating in Pakistan. The pressure India faced from the Western media, political leaders and officials falling for the 'South Asia as a nuclear flashpoint' narrative overlooked the terrorism heaped upon India and its people from across the border.

12

IC 814 Hijacking: December 1999[1]

Background

Half the world was preparing for Christmas eve on 24 December 1999. Churches across the eastern hemisphere were busy with arrangements for the midnight mass. At 4.30 p.m. local time on that fateful day, an Indian Airlines flight IC 814 took off routinely from Kathmandu Airport in Nepal. Piloted by a young captain Devi Sharan, it carried 191 passengers, including twenty-four foreign nationals and fifteen crew members. It was scheduled to land in New Delhi a couple of hours later.

Halfway through the flight when the Airbus 320 aircraft was flying in the Indian airspace over the city of Lucknow in the Indian state of Uttar Pradesh, a masked man supported by four other masked ones took over the aircraft in mid-air and forced

---

[1] This chapter has been written by the author's husband, A.R. Ghanashyam. The first-person voice in this chapter is his.

156

the captain to fly westwards. The details of the five hijackers revealed later were: (i) Ibrahim Athar alias 'Chief', a resident of Bahawalpur, Pakistan, (ii) Shahid Akhtar Sayed alias 'Doctor', a resident of Gulshan Iqbal, Karachi, Pakistan, (iii) Sunny Ahmed Qazi alias 'Burger', a resident of Defence Area, Karachi, Pakistan, (iv) Mistri Zahoor Ibrahim aka Zia, a resident of Akhtar Colony, Karachi, Pakistan and (v) Shakir, from Sukkur City, Pakistan. All of them were traced to the outfit Harkat-ul-Mujahideen (HuM), a Pakistan-based terror outfit. The then Prime Minister of India, Atal Bihari Vajpayee, told the media that there was evidence of Pakistan's involvement in the hijacking of IC 814. The harrowing experience of the passengers and crew of the hijacked aircraft continued for the next seven days. Entire India, in particular the families of passengers and crew on board IC 814, remained glued to television screens watching the saga of the hijacked aircraft. The world at large, too, followed the story.

Once they got hold of the aircraft, the hijackers sought to land it in Lahore in order to replenish its depleting fuel. Lahore was home turf for them after all. But the airport control tower refused permission for landing. Capt. Sharan then managed to persuade the hijackers that Amritsar across the border in India was the only option available. The aircraft then flew to Amritsar and landed there at 7 p.m. seeking fuel. The hijackers waited anxiously for forty-five minutes for fuel in vain. They must have got further intrigued when the fuel bowser, which had started towards the aircraft speedily, suddenly stopped some distance away. The long delay and abrupt stoppage of the bowser may have accentuated the anxiety of the hijackers, and they forced the captain to take off from Amritsar at 7.50 p.m. without refuelling.

Landing IC 814 in Amritsar could not have been in the hijackers' game plan. Why would they hijack an Indian Aircraft and take the risk of landing in another Indian airport three hours later giving Indian authorities a clear chance to mount a rescue operation? Be that as it may, when refuelling was not taking place even after several minutes of waiting, they must have asked the pilot to take off, threatened him that they will kill the passengers if he didn't and finally compelled him to take off without refuelling. Unfortunately, the window of opportunity for India passed by and the bird flew away from Amritsar.

Much has been revealed and written about what happened in the IC 814 episode in its Amritsar leg. The important question is: why did the aircraft not wait for fuel? The captain had a fantastic opportunity to refuse to fly in the name of an empty fuel tank. I quote his answer to V.P. Haran during the return flight from Kandahar to New Delhi on 31 December. Haran was then a director in the Ministry of External Affairs, who had accompanied External Affairs Minister Jaswant Singh to Kandahar.

To quote Haran:

I asked the pilot Mr. Sharan, why he took off from Amritsar. He said that the hijackers told him to take the plane to Lahore and that he had told them there is very little fuel and he can't reach any airport. Then they stabbed a passenger and brought the knife dripping with blood and told him that every 10 minutes they will kill a passenger till the flight takes off. The pilot did not know if the passenger who was stabbed was alive or not. The hijacker came again with the blood-stained knife and repeated his earlier threat. The pilot said he then took a calculated risk to fly to Lahore as he did not want innocent passengers to be stabbed to death. Lahore airport did not give permission for the flight to land despite his informing the control tower that he was very low on fuel and that he can't fly back to Amritsar. Still the refusal stood. He told them he was landing anyway; then they switched off the landing lights and the airport lights. It was with great difficulty that he could identify the runway and land the aircraft, with fuel left for just about 35 seconds of flight. If he had failed to spot the runway it would have been a far greater disaster.

The refuelled aircraft took off from Lahore around 10.30 p.m. local time. It landed around 3 a.m. local time at Al Minhad Military Airbase, 25 km from the bustling International Airport of Dubai. It was here that twenty-seven women and children, from among 176 passengers, were released. The body of Rupin Katyal, killed on board IC 814 when stabbed by a hijacker, was also handed over at Dubai. A relief Indian Airlines airplane brought home the released passengers and the remains of Katyal.

I have heard several different accounts of how Katyal got killed. One was that when all the passengers had been ordered to remain seated with their heads down, he raised his head either involuntarily or out of curiosity. A hijacker forced him with a knife at his throat to the executive class. On the way, he was wounded and subsequently bled to death. Another was quoted in a story published on a website Soapboxie in October 2022 in which one Ashutosh Joshi writes, 'In order to create panic, they (hijackers) stabbed one of the passengers, Rupin Katyal (25), first in the abdomen then in the chest a number of times. At this stage, the helpless Captain was forced to take off without refuelling.'[2] Yet another version is of YouTuber Dhruv Rathee.[3] In his video of January 2023, he says that one Satnam Singh was stabbed in Amritsar to persuade the captain to fly out where the flight had landed for refuelling. Katyal must have been killed subsequently.

---

[2] Ashutosh Joshi, 'The Hijack of Flight IC 814', SoapBoxie, 22 October 2022.

[3] Mystery of Flight IC 814 | The Worst Plane Hijacking in Indian History | Dhruv Rathee, YouTube

When the aircraft took off from Lahore, it could have landed in an Afghan airport but there was no night navigation in Afghanistan. At that time, New Delhi was still grappling with possibilities of where the aircraft was headed. When it flew towards the Middle East, K.C. Singh, the then Indian envoy to the United Arab Emirates, used his personal contacts to let the plane land in Dubai, writes Manvendra Singh, Jaswant Singh's son. He adds that after much cajoling, the commander of the UAE Air Force and Air Defence, Mohammed bin Zayed al-Nahyan, allowed the IC 814 to land at the Al Minhad Air Base.

The aircraft left Al Minhad Air Base in Dubai with the remaining passengers, crew and hijackers. It landed in Kandahar, Afghanistan, at 8.55 a.m. on Christmas Day, 1999. There, it stayed put till the last day of the last year of the previous millennium; it was 1 January 2000 when it finally returned to New Delhi.

December 1999: Islamabad

In the evening of 24 December, Shahid Khan, Press Trust of India (PTI) correspondent in Islamabad, Pakistan, informed High Commissioner Gopalaswamy Parthasarathy that the Indian Airlines flight IC 814 that took off from Kathmandu and which was scheduled to land in New Delhi had been hijacked in Indian airspace. Parthasarathy must have realized that the Mission in Pakistan will be dragged into the episode sooner than later going by past precedents. He summoned all the officers to the Chancery for a meeting to bring everyone up to date. As was feared, the aircraft did head to Lahore. The high commissioner was to be flown from the air force base in Islamabad to Lahore. Before he could proceed, news came that the aircraft had left Lahore. We opened a logbook in the High Commission and started recording regular situation reports and kept following the news. We were informed the next day that IC 814 had landed in Kandahar at 8.55 a.m.

* * *

It was 26 December 1999. My wife Ruchi and I were watching Television News at our home in Islamabad. The telephone rang. It was 10 p.m., the night was chilly and the air was still. The high commissioner summoned both of us to his residence, the India House. We reached almost immediately; India House was right next to our residence, with only a compound between us in block F-7 of Islamabad. We just walked across. A tray of tea with some nuts and biscuits was kept on the centre table. Without wasting any time the high commissioner said, 'The government has decided to send Ghanashyam to Kandahar.'

For a few seconds, there was silence in the room. Several questions started whirring in my mind. At the outset, I dealt with neither the political desk nor the security aspects in the Mission. In fact, I worked on totally unrelated issues of Trade and Economy. The first question, therefore, was why I was detailed for Kandahar. The second was: What am I supposed to do there? Am I to get in touch with the hijackers and, if so, what would I ask them or tell them? Third, how long would I be gone? I did raise these questions, but no one including, the high commissioner himself, knew the answers.

I had read about the ruthless manner in which the Taliban conducted their policy of implementing Islamic Shariat. In August 1998, they had hacked ten Iranian diplomats and an Iranian journalist in the city of Mazar-i-Sharif in Afghanistan. By then, I had already seen several reports of gruesome violence in Afghanistan. Be that as it may, for some inexplicable reason, I was curious and may be even excited than being worried or scared about being sent to the Taliban land.

The high commissioner concluded the meeting after informing me that a UN plane will take me to Kandahar and that I would have to be at the Islamabad Airport by dawn on 27 December 1999.

We returned home, with both of us buried in thought about what lay ahead. Our two young sons were asleep. I packed my clothes and put in some woollens to see me through the single-digit temperature in Kandahar. By hand, I carried a rainproof overcoat with faux fur-lining inside. In my briefcase I had my basic toiletries, a warm grey pashmina shawl, a 200-page exercise notebook, and some pens and pencils. The notebook became my prized possession since I kept my notes in it. Although nobody had asked me to keep notes, I thought to myself that I may never again witness such an extraordinary event and decided to chronologically record each development.

I left home in the wee hours of the morning of 27 December in a limousine of the Indian High Commission. When I reached the Islamabad Airport, it was still dark. The immigration formalities were completed after some wait. Officials from the airport then escorted me to the small UN aircraft. A short ladder with half-a-dozen steps was in position for me to board the aircraft. With my overcoat and briefcase, I entered the empty aircraft and sat on a seat close to the door. It had some ten or twelve seats with only the cockpit crew and one technician.

By the time the aircraft took off, it was well past sunrise. The airport looked simply beautiful, swept in the golden rays of the morning sun. Once airborne, I kept looking at the landscape of mountains, some green and some snowclad, and fields without much vegetation. During the entire flight, there was nobody to talk to. I tried to remain calm and took periodic deep breaths. I kept my mind blank and avoided thinking about what the day had on offer for me.

After about three hours, the aircraft commenced its descent. When we landed and the aircraft began skiing on the long and never-ending runway, I saw to my left abandoned cannibalized aircraft, vehicles and bits and pieces of steel and rubber strewn all along. That was indeed a whole lot of junk and huge amount of steel. Finally, the aircraft came to a standstill. The door opened and the descending ladder was let down. When I stood at the door of the aircraft, my eyes went straight to the IC 814 Airbus parked perhaps about 150 metres away, with all its window shutters down. I then looked down and noticed two people standing at the edge of the ladder—a tall white gentleman and another who looked shorter perhaps because he was next to a tall one. The tall person was the head of the UN Office for the Coordination of Humanitarian Affairs (OCHA). The other was wearing a white Afghan tunic and a sleeveless black jacket, gold-rimmed glasses and a shining black turban with a long tail that flowed out of the turban at the back. It was Wakil Ahmad Mutawakil, Taliban foreign minister. With a diffident smile I shook hands with both, wished the representative of OCHA 'good morning and happy to meet you' and greeted the Taliban foreign minister with the traditional Islamic greeting— 'Assalaamu Alaikum'. I then excused myself to go to the washroom. It was a long flight and there was no toilet in the aircraft. Outside the airport lounge, I could only see three washrooms, each with a pot, a sink and a little space for ablutions and bathing. I wondered later how so many journalists, cameramen and diplomats of countries whose nationals were passengers in the hijacked plane managed with such minimal facilities.

Mutawakil was unsure of how to deal with me. He spoke Pushtu and I didn't. I spoke English, but he was not comfortable in it. I could feel the anxiety in the eyes and tones of both gentlemen when they told me that I should straightaway get in touch with my interlocutors in the aircraft. The OCHA representative added, 'The plane arrived in Kandahar two days ago and those in control inside the aircraft are extremely angry and annoyed with the Government of India for the delay in the commencement of negotiations.' It was the month of Ramadan, when religious Muslims fast during the day, eating only after sunset and before the following sunrise. That must have made them even more irritable.

Someone took the footage as I was descending from the short ladder of the UN aircraft in Kandahar in the forenoon of 27 December. This footage and a photograph of the parked IC 814 Airbus 320 aircraft were by far the two templates used continuously by the Indian and international media. Out of the blue 'an Indian diplomat A.R. Ghanashyam, Counsellor in the Indian High Commission in Islamabad, reaches Kandahar' became the headline. I had no idea; although there were several journalists and any number of still picture cameras and video cameras outside the airport lounge, I had no access to television news channels. The days of ubiquitous smartphones were still years away and communication was mostly through the most expensive satellite phones.

The time I spent in Kandahar must also have been an anxious period for my own family, including my wife, our two little boys, colleagues and close friends. A host of near and dear ones from schools and colleges where I studied and offices where I had worked suddenly realized that they recognized me. Some would tell me years later, when I got to meet them, how excited they were to suddenly see me on television on that occasion. In Ajjampur, my little place of birth in Karnataka, one newspaper's headline announced proudly in Kannada: 'Karnataka's son in Kandahar'. Strangely, very few seemed to have realized that my life could have been at risk out there in Kandahar.

I was escorted to the control tower of the airport by a burly gentleman who managed to communicate with me in broken English and Urdu. Much later, I would learn that it was Akhtar Mohammad Mansour, then in-charge of aviation and air force facility at Kandahar. He was also the Corps Commander of Kandahar (CCK).

I climbed the many steps to reach the cabin at the top of the control tower along with CCK. I felt cramped inside the cabin, which had all kinds of machines and equipment. Once I reached, I was given a microphone with a speaker in front of me. The officer in-charge of the control tower informed the aircraft that the first Indian official had arrived and was in the control tower ready to establish contact with the interlocutors in the aircraft. I was straightaway in touch on voice, not face to face, with one of the hijackers—their designated communicator.

For me personally, it had been a long and anxious wait for this moment. I wished my interlocutor '*Assalamu Alaikum*'. In his enthusiasm to pounce on me, he forgot to return my greetings and went on a long, winding harangue about the 'excesses of the Indian armed forces in Kashmir' and how 'inhuman and deplorable was the treatment being meted out to the people of Kashmir by the Indian government'. He sat on a high horse and sermonized with great elan. He may have had his last meal before sunrise, as per religious practice in the month of Ramadan, which was at least seven to eight hours ago. He still had the energy to speak loud and clear in chaste Urdu. 'The more he speaks, the more time I gain and that is good,' I thought to myself. I realized that there was no point in getting irritated and countering his allegations, which would have further excited and emboldened him to become more difficult than what he already was. Thinking that discretion was the better part of valour, I didn't interrupt or immediately respond.

When he seemed to have tired out and fell silent, I asked him quietly in Urdu, 'Janab, do you have any message for me to communicate to my government?' That seemed to infuriate him no end and he started shouting again, 'What kind of country are you? What kind of government do you have? Here we are, waiting for more than two days for your delegation to get in touch with us. Don't you care for the lives of people inside the aircraft who are your citizens? If there is any further delay, I will start killing passengers one by one and every hour you will have a new body thrown on the tarmac. Are you prepared for it? Are you listening to me?'

I realized that the situation was turning serious and could easily go out of hand. I constantly reminded myself that these wretched men had come prepared to die if need be. They had all the protection and I had none. They had nothing to lose, and I had everything, including the passengers and the aircraft, to lose. I was painfully aware that the aircraft that was to transport the Indian delegation from New Delhi had developed some technical glitch and a new aircraft had to be organized which had taken some extra time.

I responded calmly, slowly and clearly in Hindi/Urdu, 'Janab, at the outset I am already here, and you are talking to me. What makes you think that there will be further delay. Our delegation is ready to board and any time they will fly out of Delhi and reach here. As you would be aware, governments have rules to abide by, procedures to follow and approvals to be obtained from concerned authorities at each step of the decision-making process. The prime minister and his cabinet are personally monitoring the situation and facilitating the decisions to expedite the departure of the delegation to Kandahar. You must have patience. Like I said earlier, am I not already here?' That is how the conversation was concluded.

When the tense exchange ended, I heaved a sigh of relief. I came out of the cabin and slowly started coming down the stairs of the control tower. The CCK followed me. My mind got thinking, 'What if the hijackers really kill passengers and start throwing the dead bodies on the tarmac?' *Shubh shubh socho!* (Think of good things), I told myself.

While we were walking towards the airport lounge, the CCK said to me in broken English, 'You know, my friend, even if we had 200 sheep on board that aircraft, we would have blown it up by now.' I responded with a smile, 'Excellency, I fully agree with you. Had there been 200 sheep on board that aircraft, we could blow it up too. Unfortunately, the passengers and crew members in that aircraft are human beings and each has a family to care for back home. How can we blow up the aircraft in such a scenario?' The CCK was perhaps satisfied with my answer and did not pursue further. We continued some small talk till we reached the airport lounge.

After we returned to the lounge, an OCHA officer quietly pushed a brown paper envelop into my hands. He said I will find it useful. When I opened the packet much later, I realized that it contained different kinds of chocolates and chocolate bars. The kind gentleman must have thought that I may not get anything to eat during the day as everyone was fasting and the chocolates would come handy to keep myself at least partially replenished in energy to survive the day.

At the lounge, I could speak a few words with Minister Muttawakil. I told him that I don't know Pushtu but can speak a little bit of Arabic. I could see a wide smile on his face. When we started speaking in Arabic, I realized that while he understood my classical (Quranic) Arabic without any difficulty, I struggled to understand his colloquial dialect of the beautiful language. But we managed, nevertheless.

I asked Muttawakil, 'Excellency, what kind of arrangements are in place as and when the passengers and crew are released?' In response, he said something in Pushtu to a young man nearby. The young man escorted me around the camp next to the lounge a few 100 metres away, where there were some tents. In each tent were people, bottles of water, medicine baskets and a makeshift bed. A few who wore white gowns did look like doctors or paramedics.

Each time I had something important to inform, like the conversations with the hijacker or the CCK or Muttawakil, I called up the HC in Islamabad using the UN phone. After a few such calls, the HC suggested that I stop calling him. For a moment I froze and felt alone, but fortunately I recovered soon enough. We both knew the risk of being monitored by intelligence agencies around when we spoke on open lines and realized that it was wiser and safer not to use insecure phones.

Arrival of the special flight in Kandahar, 27 December 1999

By around 4.30 p.m., an Indian Airlines special aircraft arrived carrying five officials of the Government of India and a ten-member squad of Indian Airlines technicians to Kandahar. The officials were C.D. Sahai and Anand Arni from the Cabinet Secretariat, Ajit Doval and Nehchal Sandhu from the Intelligence Bureau and Vivek Katju, joint secretary heading the Pakistan, Iran and Afghanistan Division of the Ministry of External Affairs. I was there to receive them. Two rooms were allocated in the guest house of Ariana Afghan Airlines a few minutes ride from the Kandahar Airport for the six of us. Sahai, Doval and Katju occupied one room and I shared the other with Arni and Sandhu.

A big issue was the dismal washroom facility. A single toilet was used by many. I would get up at 3 a.m. and get ready before the rush began. I recall one day, when our toilet was occupied, I asked the old caretaker at the guest house if there was another washroom nearby that I could use as I was running late. He showed me another building a few metres away. I went across with my towel and toilet bag and used a bathroom there. I found the occupants of that place very different from Afghans; they also did not have the traditional Afghan headgear. I casually mentioned it to Katju. He also went across and sauntered around the place. We were both more than convinced that the other building was occupied by non-Afghan outsiders from across the border assisting or supervising the Taliban in the IC 814 episode.

The one who communicated from among the five hijackers spoke chaste Urdu. We really did not need interpretation for the Indian team, as all members followed Hindi and Urdu reasonably well. But each time we needed to consult the Taliban or wanted them to intervene in the negotiations, either to clarify the hijackers' demands or to address our own reservations about them or wanted to break a deadlock, we needed an interpreter. That is how young Sayed Rehmatullah Hashemi arrived on the scene. He spoke six languages: Dari, Pushto, Persian, Urdu, English and Arabic.

I recall an interesting superstition that is prevalent in Afghanistan which Hashmi narrated to me. When an Afghan child did not start speaking even after more than two years of age, his mother would take the child to a Sikh family and let the lady of that household feed the child with roti made by her. Soon thereafter, the child would start speaking and develop fluency. Hashmi told me about this belief in Afghanistan and added that he himself happened to be one such child. Hashemi improved steadily thereafter and was now speaking six languages with ease.

IC 814 was hijacked four days ago; the aircraft with the passengers, crew and the hijackers had since landed and taken off from three other airports: Amritsar, Lahore and Al Minhad Dubai, before landing in Kandahar two days ago. The Government in New Delhi, and Prime Minister Atal Bihari Vajpayee personally, were under enormous pressure, particularly from the families of passengers onboard flight IC 814. We were running against time. Obviously, we wanted to commence negotiations forthwith. But while we knew our demands, the hijackers hadn't revealed theirs and we needed that crucial input to begin the process of negotiations. A request was sent forthwith to the aircraft.

When we received the green signal, some of us went across to the aircraft. When we approached the aircraft door, it gingerly opened, and a piece of paper was dropped from the aircraft. A cool wind gushed past, and it was blown away from us. It was a page carefully torn from a lined exercise notebook. I ran after the flying piece of paper and finally laid my hands on it. The first thing I noticed on seeing it was the beautiful calligraphic handwriting in which the demands had been written. We came back to the lounge with the precious document.

The Taliban had provided one room in the building adjacent to the airport lounge for the Indian delegation. The hijackers remained ensconced in the aircraft. We had our radio communication equipment, and they used the aircraft's radio. The objectives of the Indian side were known: (i) to get the passengers and crew safely released along with their baggage, (ii) take over the aircraft and (iii) minimize the demands of the hijackers in lieu of (i) and (ii), in that order. Under the main objective of getting the passengers released, the priority was to get any remaining children, women, elderly and sick passengers out.

The hijackers operated from a position of advantage, as they had the sympathy and protection of the Taliban locally and from the authorities across the border in Pakistan. The one disadvantage they had was that they did not eat during the day since it was the holy Islamic month of Ramadan, when pious Muslims fast from sunrise to sunset. They were, thus, easily tired by the long negotiations. The Indian delegation, however, was a sitting duck, with no protection but for the courtesies extended by the hosts. The reality was that we had no diplomatic relations with Afghanistan those days and were nevertheless the guests of the Taliban regime in Kandahar.

The list of demands written down neatly on the page of an exercise notebook brought from the hijackers had thirty-eight items. Thirty-six were convicts arrested in India for various crimes, and the hijackers wanted them released. Without exception they were all Pakistani nationals. One other demand was about the remains of Sajjad Afghani, the founder of Harkat-ul-Mujahideen (HuM) who had been buried in India. The hijackers wanted his body to be exhumed and returned. The last but not the least in importance was $200 million in hundred-dollar bills. It was a long list, and negotiations began on the morning of 27 December.

By this time, the airport lounge was filled with what seemed like hundreds of journalists from across the world and several diplomats who had arrived to touch base with the passengers, who were their nationals, whenever that became possible. They were witnessing how the episode unravelled.

When the first lunch came in, it was a packet containing one big Afghan naan bread, a roasted chicken leg, one slice of cucumber and another of onion. Even that was a boon because the others around us were not eating. After a few of those meals, we started getting some kind of packed meals from across the border in Pakistan at an exorbitant price. The joke going around among the people at the lounge was that the sudden arrival of so many people in Kandahar meant that the little town, which then had just about 2,90,000 people, had run out of chicken.

The demand for exhuming Afghani's remains was not an easy one to implement. At our request, the Taliban supported the argument that such an act would be untenable in Islam. After a long debate, the demand was eventually dropped. The same logic was applied to the demand for US dollar currency bills. After several arguments and counter arguments, that demand was also removed from the list.

I periodically sauntered near and in the lounge where journalists and diplomats stayed, just to make them feel comfortable under the extraordinary circumstance. Every time I came out of the negotiating room during breaks and went across to them, I had to deal with their questions. I would simply tell them that negotiations were going on and everyone must wait till the end for the outcome. At one time, I told an Indian journalist to the effect that the process was in progress and there must be some give and take while moving towards the final resolution. That got splashed as the headline in the next day's newspapers. I did raise my guard thereafter in dealing with journalists.

In addressing the other demands on the release of thirty-six prisoners, the position the delegation took was that at the outset we did not know where these prisoners were held—which jails in which districts of what provinces in the vast geography of India. The first step was to collect and compile that crucial information. It couldn't be done overnight and would take time. Second, these prisoners couldn't be taken out of their jails and brought to Kandahar just like that. There were cases pending against them in Indian courts of law. Justification for their release would have to be explained to the concerned courts of law and their agreement for the release of those prisoners obtained. Third, we had to work out the logistics of getting them together and transporting them to Kandahar. This process could as well take weeks, months or even longer to execute.

Arguments went backwards and forward, as well as for and against. There were occasions when negotiations came to a grinding halt and both sides went back to square one, to start afresh. It was frustrating but had to be done, and it was done.

Three days of continuous negotiations exhausted both sides. The negotiator from the hijackers' side, who did the speaking talking on an empty stomach day after day, was getting tired. His voice was becoming weaker by the day and the number of demands also kept reducing. By the end of the third day, the demands from the aircraft came down to the release of three prisoners: Masood Azhar, Amhed Omar Saeed Sheikh and Mushtaq Ahmed Zargar.

Kandahar, 31 December 1999

By the evening of 30 December, there was consensus and hope that the end of the ordeal was in sight. There was exhaustion on all sides although much more on the hijackers' side, as they were in a far worse physical condition inside the aircraft. There was no indication that demands could be further whittled down. Finally, the government in New Delhi came under enormous pressure to bring the passengers back home.

The night of 30 December, I sat down to work out the logistics for the next day's operations. The hijacked aircraft was standing there. The auxiliary engine, which under normal circumstances worked for some twenty hours, had miraculously lasted over 100 hours. It had kept the aircraft's air conditioning, lighting and communication equipment running. In addition, we had the second aircraft that had brought the officials and Indian Airlines' technicians. The following day, we were expecting the third, with the three terrorists being released.

There was only a single ladder appropriate for the Airbus 300 series at the airport in Kandahar for the embarkation and disembarkation of passengers. The first step was to position the ladder with the third aircraft arriving on 31 December to bring down the three terrorists and accompanying aircraft staff and officials. Second, we had to move the ladder to the hijacked IC 814 aircraft to facilitate the disembarkation of the five hijackers followed by passengers and crew from that aircraft. Third, the ladder then had to be moved to the second aircraft that arrived on 27 December and then to the third one that would bring the three released prisoners on 31 December. Both aircraft would be used to accommodate the released passengers and crew of the hijacked aircraft.

The aircraft with the three prisoners arrived in the evening of 31 December. External Affairs Minister Jaswant Singh, accompanied by other officials, was also on this aircraft. It landed just as the sun was about to set—at around 5 p.m. We followed the drill meticulously with only one change necessitated because the hijackers wanted to confirm that the released passengers were the same three they had sought. Singh and V.P. Haran, director, Ministry of External Affairs, were deplaned first from the third aircraft and taken to a separate location to meet with the Taliban foreign minister and other officials. There, Singh thanked the Taliban authorities for the courtesies extended to the passengers, the crew, the officials and the technicians who were in Kandahar for several days.

I was surprised and satisfied that there was no commotion and no mess-up. Once the three prisoners were brought down one by one, they were received by the Taliban representatives. The hijackers joined the three prisoners, following which all of them disappeared. Then, the passengers, totally exhausted but very happy to be out of the stinking aircraft, disembarked. We moved them into the other two aircraft. By the time all the operations were complete the sun had set, and it was dark. They left a couple of hours post sunset.

One of the hijackers had quietly informed Doval that a New Year's gift had been left behind in the IC 814 aircraft for the Government of India. Such news would have spread total panic, but fortunately not many had access to this information.

Jaswant Singh rang me up that night after reaching Delhi that I should not go back to the guest house where, for once, I would have been alone at night with the luxury of an entire toilet just for myself, had I returned. He insisted that I stay back in the lounge along with whoever was left there.

What happened in Kandahar after the passengers and crew and government officials departed was separately recorded by me and sent to the Ministry of External Affairs. Although it was classified, Singh reproduced a part of the report in his book *A Call to Honour*. Since it is already in the open domain, I reproduce below the extract from that book, with a few minor typographic corrections:

THE FINAL PUZZLE

The hijacked aircraft could not be taken out of Kandahar the same evening. I had received an alarm that it was planted with something that would blow up at midnight. I could not risk the lives of the relief pilots and crew. Besides it had to be checked technically before take-off. The aircraft had been kept confined for eight days. There was also the 'mystery of the red bag'. What was this 'red bag'? Who owned it? Why did the hijackers come back to recover it? The mystery cleared after Muttavakil's arrest by the United States following the defeat of the Taliban in 2001. The 'red bag' belonged to one of the hijackers, it contained explosives and, possibly, the real passports, too. In their hurry they had forgotten it in the hold. By the time they came back to recover it, the hostages had been released. Yet Muttavakil himself acted illegally, betrayed our trust, and got the hold forcibly opened, and all the red bags taken out. It is all there in the report of A.R. Ghanashyam, the diplomat sent to Kandahar from Islamabad. I share an extract:

Winding up of the visit to Kandahar

I stayed back at Kandahar to arrange the refuelling and return of the hijacked IC 814 aircraft. A crew of 13 members, including one flight engineer and two pilots – Capt JRD Rao, deputy managing director of Indian Airlines, and Capt Suri of Indian Airlines also remained in Kandahar. While the hand baggage of passengers on board IC 814 were taken by passengers themselves to the two new aircraft, their baggage in the hold had remained in the hold of the aircraft. I went on board the aircraft at 1900 hrs. The interior had an unbearable stink. The cockpit panel had left over chicken bones, peeled skin of fruits and other dirt. Toilets were choked and unusable.

I returned to the lounge and sat down for a while when I had occasion to meet Syed Rehmatullah Hashmi, our Pushto

English interpreter. We sat down in a corner of the lounge. On that occasion, I asked Hashmi what the Taliban wanted to do with the three released prisoners and the five hijackers. He said that all of them would be put in a vehicle and that vehicle would be escorted by two armed vehicles—one in the front and one at the back—till the Pakistan border. He also said that they would not be using any of the normal border passage routes but one of those Pak-Afghan secret routes the Mujahideen used during Russian occupation, where there would be no border formalities like immigration and customs. When I asked him whether at any time, Taliban were distressed enough to consider storming the plane, he said that while the inevitability of such a course of action was discussed in the beginning it was shelved once I arrived on the scene and it became known that India was sending its negotiating team. He offered to host me if I visited Quetta while he is there.

At around 2100 hours, Capt Suri came to the lounge and conveyed to me that the Taliban were not prepared to let IC 814 fly and they were delaying the refuelling and were also keen to take out one bag that belonged to the hijackers. Mr Muttawakil was still in the airport, and I rushed to him with Capt Suri and apprised him of the problem and requested him to advise the authorities to assist us in facilitating an early departure of the aircraft. At that time, I also came to know that one of the hijackers had mentioned that they had left a 'millennium present for government of India on board the aircraft'. I advised Capt Suri that we better vacate the plane and get back to the lounge. But the Taliban authorities were still trying to see the hold and look for a red suitcase of the hijackers. I brought this to the notice of Foreign Secretary (FS) and Joint Secretary (JS) Iran, Pakistan, Afghanistan (IPA) who had already reached New Delhi along with the passengers and other members of the delegation. I was advised that I should ensure that the crew and the two relief captains are not found anywhere near the aircraft and that I should also make sure that everybody stayed in one place and sleeps over in the lounge along with other diplomats, journalists, and UN staff till the next morning.

Around 2300 hrs, I found that Capt Rao had still not returned. When I looked around for Capt Suri and asked him where Capt Rao was, he told me that he was still there in the aircraft and was refusing to come back. I rushed with Capt Suri to the aircraft. It was at that time that I found the red Pajero (used by Muttawakil in Kandahar) parked right in front of the hold with its head lights focused on the door of the aircraft's hold. It could not be confirmed as to who was in the vehicle as it had tinted glasses. Capt Rao had started the engine with a jet starter and the Auxiliary Power Unit was still running. Some workers were working in the hold. Capt Rao told me at that time that he had seen people taking every red bag from the hold and showing it to the car and then taking it back to the hold. Two and two put together, we both felt that perhaps either one or more of the hijackers or someone close to them who could identify the infamous red suitcase were comfortably parked in that red Pajero car and were trying out every red bag to identify the real bag and take it out.

Capt Suri found out from a local worker that they had found one bag and there were five grenades in it. The Control tower also told the captain that the minister for civil aviation had cleared the aircraft about 15 minutes before midnight and had said that they could leave if they wanted. At any rate, the requisite fuel was still not in the tank. The aircraft had 14 tonnes of fuel and needed another 16 to 18 tonnes before it could safely take off. Finally, I was able to bring back Capt Rao and we all stayed in the lounge for the night. The next morning fuel was supplied to the plane, the engine was checked, and it took off at 0943 hrs, Afghan time. The departure of the flight was conveyed to FS at the same time.

1 January 2000

The entire Taliban officialdom never returned to the airport on the New Year's Day. I sent a message through the airport manager that I wished to see anyone from amongst the minister of civil aviation or the minister for foreign affairs or a Taliban representative to thank them and to take over the hijacker's bag. The airport manager consulted his seniors and came back to tell me that no one could be contacted. Then I insisted that if they were not likely to come to the airport, I could go and see them in the city which was about an hour from the airport. I did not receive a satisfactory answer even for this request. Around 1000 hrs, I was told that Corps Commander of Kandahar (CCK) and Syed Rehmatullah Hashmi would come to see me off and I could meet them at that time. I waited for them and even missed the first UN flight to Islamabad which took off at 1030 hrs. I was practically alone in the place with most of the remaining diplomats and UN staff having taken the first flight. Around 1100 hrs, while I was still waiting for CCK and Hashmi, one of the young officials of the control tower who spoke English, came and whispered in my ear that nobody was likely to come to see me and no one knew what had happened to the bag after it was unloaded and taken to the city. He also handed over a packet containing some almonds and raisins, a pocket comb, a nail cutter, a handkerchief, a pair of nylon socks and few meters of cotton material for an Afghan Tunic with a design on its chest and trouser like Pyjama, saying that the minister for Civil Aviation had sent these for me because he knew that I never had time to go to the city throughout my stay at the airport in Kandahar.

I boarded the second UN plane at 1200 hrs and returned to Islamabad at around 1500 hrs.[4]

Postscript

The IC 814 story would be incomplete without the three dreaded criminals released by India on 31 December 1999 during the negotiations.

The first was Masood Azhar. He was born in July 1968 at Bahawalpur in the Punjab province of Pakistan as the third of eleven children of a schoolteacher/cleric. He had some initial schooling before shifting to a religious school and graduating from it in 1989. He was arrested in 1994 while on a visit to India on a Portuguese passport, to settle some disputes between different factions of the Harkat-ul-Ansar (HuA). A high-value asset, several attempts were made to secure his release by his mentors. His proxies abducted five foreign trekkers in south Kashmir in 1995 and held them hostage, demanding his release, which was rejected by the authorities. He remained in captivity in Kot Bhalwal prison on the outskirts of Jammu before his release was finally secured in 1999.

In 2000, he founded the Jaish-e-Mohammed (JeM), a new terror outfit to wage war against India. He is believed to be the mastermind of the attack on the Indian Parliament on 13 December 2001, with seven casualties and eighteen people injured. He is mentioned as one of the key conspirators of the Pathankot Airbase attack on 2 January 2016. Although the JeM is a terrorist outfit, Masood Azhar has been able to live as a free man in Pakistan, while pursuing new methods of waging 'jihad' against India. The Chinese veto at the UN saved him from being

---

[4] Jaswant Singh, *A Call to Honour: In Service of Emergent India*, Rupa Publications, New Delhi, 2006, pp. 243–47.

listed as a designated terrorist until 1 May 2019, when he was listed as an international terrorist by the UN Security Council. Pakistani authorities occasionally put him under house arrest to mislead the world.

Ahmed Omar Saeed Sheikh was born in London in December 1973. He is the eldest child of a Pakistani clothing merchant in the UK. He was schooled in elite schools and even enrolled in the London School of Economics but dropped out after the first year. He was closely associated with terrorist outfits in and out of Pakistan, including the Al-Qaeda and the Taliban.

In India, Omar Sheikh abducted an American and three British tourists in 1994. He was arrested in a shoot-out by Indian authorities. He met Masood Azhar in prison. After Omar Sheikh's release in December 1999, he was arrested in Pakistan in 2002 and was sentenced to death for kidnapping and beheading reporter Daniel Pearl, South Asia bureau chief of the *Wall Street Journal*. Another report says he provided $100,000 to Mohamed Atta, one of the conspirators of 9/11 who flew the hijacked airliner into the World Trade Center towers in New York.

Mushtaq Ahmed Zargar, the other terrorist released on 31 December 1999, was born in 1967. He grew up in Srinagar valley and joined the Jammu and Kashmir Liberation Front in 1988. After training in Pakistan-occupied Kashmir, he returned to Jammu and Kashmir in 1989. He was involved in the 12 December 1989 kidnapping of Rubaiya Sayeed, daughter of Mufti Mohammad Sayeed, then the home minister of India. The kidnappers demanded the release of five of their comrades in exchange for her release, which was complied with. Over the years, there are reports of three dozen murder cases registered against Zargar in Srinagar. He was arrested on 15 May 1992 and imprisoned.

The year 2024 will mark twenty-five years since IC 814 was hijacked. India learnt a good deal in the saga of IC 814 but the hard way. Many rules have since been reworked and security architecture strengthened and made foolproof. Punishment regime for hijackers has been made severe and stringent. Mercifully, we have not had any hijack of an Indian aircraft since December 1999, and it has been a quarter of a century of secure airspace. Be that as it may, it cannot be presumed that future perpetrators will not keep their mission above their lives, or that chances of a repeat of such attacks and assaults are zero. In the neighbourhood we live in, India can let its guard down only at its peril.

13

IC 814 Hijacking: The Perspective from Islamabad

The evening of 31 December 1999 had finally arrived—the last day of the century. It was surreal to think that a day later would mark the beginning of not just a new year but a new century. Throughout the year, there had been concerns about the Y2K problem, and the possible havoc if the global software system could not cope with the change of date from 'ninety-nine' to 'double zero' when the year changed from 1999 to 2000.

These thoughts were far from my mind on New Year's Eve as I prepared for a small get together at India House, residence of the Indian high commissioner. I was going alone as Ghanashyam would spend the last evening of the century at Kandahar airport in Afghanistan after the release and departure of the passengers of the hijacked Indian Airlines flight IC 814.

It was dark when I got out of the house, but it was a short walk to India House. There was always a set of intelligence personnel stationed at the corner of our street.

I saw the Pakistani agent standing outside our gate as I came out. Unlike his predecessor, this agent was often insolent. That evening was no different. 'Happy New Year,' he called out behind me, his greeting sounding more like a catcall. I turned the corner and rushed into India House.

New Year's eve at India House was a subdued event. A few of the officers who were left behind in Islamabad had come with their wives. We would have dinner together, wish each other at midnight and leave. Everyone present was conscious that my husband would spend that night in Kandahar, as the Indian team had already reached Delhi with the hijacked passengers. Jaswant Singh, then external affairs minister, had asked Ghanashyam not to return to the guest house where he and the negotiating team had been staying. He did not have access to a phone at the Kandahar airport, and we could not reach him and ascertain his safety or wish him for New Year.

Shanti Parthasarathy, the high commissioner's lovely wife, was our gracious and charming hostess. We were good friends and took our morning walks together. She was also my shopping companion. The two of us would often escape to Sunday markets together in my car, leaving our respective husbands behind. Unfettered by spousal disapproval, we invariably ended up buying souvenirs that we didn't need.

Knowing me well, she sensed my disquiet and tried her best to keep us all cheerful. Her sunny disposition and affectionate nature kept us in good humour, but the conversation eventually turned to the hijacking.

Other passenger flights had been hijacked from India to Lahore or Karachi in the past. In January 1971, the Srinagar to Jammu Indian Airlines passenger flight named Ganga was hijacked[1] to Lahore by two hijackers, Hashim Qureshi and his cousin, Ashraf Qureshi of the National Liberation Front. The passengers were released, but the plane was burnt down. In September 1976, another Indian Airlines plane was hijacked from Delhi by a group of six terrorists.[2] The hijackers were caught after being served with water laced with colourless tranquillizer at Lahore, where they had landed for refuelling for their journey ahead, apparently to Libya, North Africa. The plane was sent back to India with eighty-three passengers onboard. In September 1981, extremists hijacked a Srinagar to Delhi flight to Lahore, but the passengers were freed in a Pakistani commando action. In July 1984, another Srinagar to Delhi flight was hijacked to Lahore, where the passengers were freed following a seventeen-hour ordeal when the hijackers surrendered to the Pakistani authorities.

In August 1984, a Chandigarh to Srinagar flight was hijacked to Lahore, Karachi and Dubai.[3] The then UAE defence minister negotiated the release of the passengers. Subsequent investigations showed that the pistol recovered from the hijacker was part of a consignment sent from Germany to a PO Box in Islamabad, though the Pakistan Foreign Office denied this. In April 1993, another Indian Airlines aircraft flying from Delhi to Srinagar via Jammu was hijacked, but Pakistan authorities refused it permission to land at Lahore. The plane landed at

---

[1] Saleem Akhtar Malik, 'The Ganga Hijacking in 1971', Global Village Space, 4 November 2022.

[2] Majid Sheikh, 'Harking back: A journalist's tale of the "hijacking" of an Indian aircraft', Dawn, 4 June 2023.

[3] 'This Day: August 26, 1984 — All passengers, crew of jet freed', Hindustan Times, 25 August 2021.

Amritsar where the hijacker was killed, and passengers were released.[4]

Given the history of hijackings of Indian Airlines flights to Lahore, we had become alert with our contingency plans soon after the news of the hijacking of IC 814 had reached us.

Being the week of Christmas and New Year, most officers had proceeded on vacation to India with their families. Among those left behind was an experienced officer and first secretary in the Mission, Mr T.R. Jatav. He had the added advantage of being adept at shorthand. He was designated the record keeper for the crisis. He did an excellent job of shadowing the high commissioner, from room to room, jotting down all important instructions and actions taken by the Mission, while taking note of every phone call, briefly recording the time, details of the caller and the content of the call. His record was invaluable. During those tense days, it was somehow reassuring to see the tall, well-built Jatav rushing behind the high commissioner, always with a notebook and pen in hand, but always calm.

Those were the days of long and tense hours in the high commission. Following Ghanashyam's departure for Kandahar, the already depleted team at the Mission was reduced even more. We had to ensure that there was always an officer at hand to attend to incoming phone calls. For a few days, I went home only to shower and freshen up. The caution was worthwhile, as late one night, the Taliban ambassador in Islamabad called when I was the only officer in the Mission.

When the high commissioner told Ghanashyam about going to Kandahar, he apologized to me saying, 'Sorry, Ruchi. There

---

[4] Details of previous hijackings are based on openly available information on the Internet, including Nikhil Inamdar, 'India's tryst with plane hijacks', *Business Standard*, 18 March 2014.

is really no one else I can send.' His concern was not misplaced. India had no relations with the Taliban. This would be India's first official contact with the Taliban. There was no way of knowing what kind of reception or treatment Ghanashyam would receive at the hands of the Taliban. That was probably the reason for sending a relatively young officer to Kandahar ahead of the team from India: He was being sent like the proverbial sacrificial lamb to test the waters in Taliban land.

This came through in the suo motu statement by the external affairs minister on 1 March 2000 in Parliament on the 'Hijacking of Indian airlines Flight IC-814':

> In view of the ideological orientation of the Taliban, their close linkage with Pakistan, their publicly expressed attitude towards Jammu & Kashmir, and their support to fundamentalist organisations, it was essential that an assessment regarding their approach towards the hijacking, the hijackers and the assistance that could be expected of them in its termination be first established. It was important that there be no misjudgement in this regard, at this critical juncture. After assessment, and as a first step, an official (Ghanashyam) from our High Commission in Islamabad was sent to Kandahar on the morning of December 27. Strengthened by his report from the spot, a team of officials, including doctors and a relief crew, reached Kandahar, from Delhi on 27th evening itself.[5]

The word 'Taliban' is the plural of the Arabic word 'Talib', which means 'a student'. The Taliban were students of Islamic schools in Pakistan, mainly the Pashtun areas, but also Balochistan and

---

[5] 'Suo Motu Statement by Minister of External Affairs in Parliament on the Hijacking of Indian Airlines Flight IC-814', 1 March 2000, Media Centre, mea.gov.in, paragraphs 11 and 12.

Karachi, as well as south and east Afghanistan. Their emergence and growth were facilitated by the chaos and civil war in Afghanistan that prevailed after the withdrawal of the Soviet Union from Afghanistan in 1988. The Taliban were deposed in the US-led 'Global War on Terror' following the 11 September (9/11) attacks on the US by the Al-Qaeda, the Osama bin Laden-led terrorist group. At the time of their defeat in December 2001, the Taliban held sway over most parts of Afghanistan, except the Panjshir valley, a guerrilla stronghold under the leadership of Ahmad Shah Massoud, popularly known as the 'Lion of Panjshir'. The Taliban made several offensives between 1996 and 2001, but Massoud and his forces successfully defended the valley each year and saved it from being overrun.

It is widely accepted that the Taliban emerged due to the support of Pakistan's military and ISI, which continued its support to them during their time in and out of power. This support strengthened the Taliban when they were out of power, helped them to regroup, and facilitated their re-emergence as the regime in power in Kabul following the US withdrawal from Afghanistan in August 2021.

Not only did the Taliban emerge from Pakistani madrasas, in the 1990s, Pakistani 'volunteers' kept the Taliban campaigns going. Every conquest added to their coffers. The new equipment and munitions they took over from territories they captured—from rifles and bullets to tanks and MiG fighters—became useful for their continued advance. Several Pakistani prisoners captured along with Taliban fighters by Mujahideen commanders were interviewed by journalists and human rights organizations. Analysts have written of training camps run for Pakistan-supported terrorist groups in Afghanistan, including for the anti-India HuM, which was behind the hijacking of the IC 814 from Kathmandu. Official denials by Pakistan had no takers.

The Pakistani establishment seemed peeved at Ghanashyam's deputation to Kandahar. A senior representative of the Pakistan Foreign Office was quoted by the Urdu press as claiming that Ghanashyam had been sent to Afghanistan as he belonged to R&AW, India's intelligence agency. The Pakistani official asked rhetorically, 'Why has he been sent to Kandahar? Is he going to negotiate a trade agreement with the Taliban?! (Ghanashyam was the commercial counsellor in the Mission. An officer of the Indian Foreign Service, he was posted to Islamabad by the Ministry of External Affairs and was not representing any intelligence agency.)

I wondered if the question reflected the incompetence of the Pakistani establishment or its ignorance about who represented the Indian intelligence agencies in the Mission. Or was it their deep-seated malice? This kind of speculation in the Urdu press heightened our general anxiety about the treatment that Ghanashyam could expect from the Taliban in Kandahar.

In January 2000, we attended a large gathering at a colleague's house that included some Pakistanis. A Pakistani friend who wrote columns for some Pakistani papers cornered me. He started asking me if Ghanashyam was the 'station chief' in Islamabad, and persisted with, 'So who's the "station chief" if it is not him?' I responded somewhat testily and a bit rudely, 'When it comes to Pakistan, we have a billion agents in India. All of us are R&AW agents!' That was the end of his probing.

A few months after the hijacking, we went to Peshawar. Early morning, on our first day in Peshawar, we went up to the historic fort in Peshawar at the recommendation of a waiter serving breakfast at the hotel's cafe. He proudly told us that the historic fort had been built by Babur and that Hari Singh Nalwa, the famous commander-in-chief of the Khalsa army of the Sikh empire, had reconstructed the fort after the Sikhs occupied Peshawar. The British East India Company reconstructed its outer wall. The fort is in the heart of Peshawar and according to the waiter, a 'must-see' tourist attraction.

We bought tickets to enter the fort with our car after showing our passports and drove around. As we were enjoying the panoramic view of Peshawar from a point close to the top of the fort, a Pakistani soldier approached us in panic and asked us to leave immediately as it was a military area. The fort has been the headquarters of Pakistan's Frontier Corps in Peshawar. As Indians, we were not allowed inside military premises. Fortunately, we had shown our passports at the entrance and could not be charged with espionage.

The next day, I met the head of an NGO devoted to the welfare of Afghan refugees in Pakistan. An Afghan himself, he started talking of how Ahmad Shah Massoud, the 'Lion of Panjshir', had managed to prevent the Taliban from gaining complete suzerainty over Afghanistan. I was surprised when he said that Massoud was a thorn in the side of the Taliban and the Pakistanis and their proteges, the Taliban, hated him. He said, 'If somehow Massoud could be taken out of the equation, all of Afghanistan would fall to the Taliban in no time.' He added that Massoud's life was in danger. I had no way of verifying his input or to judge if his caution was just speculation or based on specific information, as he refused to say anything further.

As events unfolded in the summer of 2000, Massoud remained ensconced in Panjshir valley until he was assassinated by Al-Qaeda linked terrorists posing as journalists on 9 September 2001, just two days before the 11 September attacks in the US. The 9/11 attacks finally led to US involvement and the defeat of the Taliban in Afghanistan. I was in Delhi in 2001 when news of Massoud's assassination became known. I couldn't help but remember the unknown Afghan who had expressed fears of Massoud's assassination a year ago in Peshawar.

A question that people frequently ask me is whether I was afraid when Ghanashyam was sent to Kandahar. Almost twenty-five years later, I sometimes wonder if I should have feared what might happen to my husband in the Taliban's den!

At the time of the hijacking, only three countries in the world recognized the Taliban regime that controlled most of Afghanistan: Pakistan, Saudi Arabia and the UAE. As the counsellor (political) at the Mission, I covered and reported on developments in Afghanistan from Islamabad. As a result, I had been writing about the gruesome nature of the Taliban regime and the many killings, floggings, etc., that were reported in the media.

Though I was aware of the violent acts in the Taliban-controlled Afghanistan and the presence of the Al-Qaeda there, I was also conscious that the Taliban were predominantly from Pashtun areas. The pre-Islamic informal code of honour, 'Pashtunwali', which is deeply ingrained in the Pashtun way of life, prohibits harming a guest in their land. Pashtun homes have offered refuge or asylum against enemies for centuries, even at the cost of their own family or fortune. Given my optimistic nature, I chose not to dwell too much on the presence of Arabs, the Al-Qaeda, or its leader Osama bin Laden and other foreign terrorists in Afghanistan. I was reassured that the Pashtun tradition of loyalty to the guest offered a measure of protection to my husband. This belief kept me calm during the last few days of 1999. In hindsight, my faith in the Taliban's attachment to 'Pashtunwali', even if misguided, was borne out by the safe return of my husband.

Our children were sleeping when Ghanashyam left for Kandahar, and I had already left for the High Commission by the time they woke up. Our younger son later wrote in an article that he learnt from the TV that his father had gone to Kandahar. Unfortunately, I was not around to counsel and reassure the children in case they got anxious, but our older son, Anant, told him not to worry and took care of his younger brother. They did not ask me any anxious questions either during or after the hijacking and from what I could make out in my brief encounters with them, they didn't seem too worried.

Were we brave or naive, or simply too busy doing our work? Twenty-five years later, I am still unsure . . .

14

Being a Woman in Islamabad

I suppressed a small yawn as I heard my friend Rubina detail her daily make-up regimen and the beauty routine she followed at night. The conversation that evening had been especially numbing, moving from ailments of children and the layers of oil required in chicken curry to the inadequacy of domestic staff. With barely suppressed boredom, I asked Rubina why she needed to follow such an elaborate beauty routine. She was a handsome woman, somewhat on the wrong side of youth but still extremely attractive. Her reply jolted me out of my ennui, as she said, 'I must try to keep looking good or my husband might bring a second wife. He is allowed four wives.'

I was suddenly face to face with the insecurity of a woman facing her fading youth. Rubina's husband was a businessman. One of his enterprises was a moving company that allowed them to be at events attended by 'Indians'. Rubina explained that in Pakistan, women of her age were apprehensive as men would often get a younger wife around the time a woman crossed her forties. 'You won't understand. This is not such a big problem in your country,' she said.

It is not that Pakistan is unique in this regard. In many societies, men can take additional wives through 'traditional marriages', while having one formal wife. In other parts of the world, men can and do have informal 'companions' outside of marriage. But in Rubina's mind, Pakistani women suffered higher levels of anxiety on this score.

Women in Pakistan did seem to have a harder struggle compared to women elsewhere. At the extreme end of the ladder seemed rural Balochistan. The Baloch educationist Samina Naz wrote in a paper, 'The status of female education in rural Balochistan presents a depressing picture. Although illiteracy in Pakistan stands at 80% and growing, the literacy rate among rural women in Balochistan is bleaker. It is estimated that less than 2% of rural female in Balochistan are literate.'[1] Analysts point out that per capita ratio of female education was lowest in Balochistan globally, while the female mortality rate was the highest in the world.[2] 'Honour killings, acid attacks, maternal mortality, and illiteracy—life for women in Pakistan's largest province is grim.'[3]

---

[1] Samina Naz, *The status of female education in rural Balochistan. Impact: Making a difference*, Aga Khan University, August 2003. Available at: http://ecommons.aku.edu/book_chapters/48; The benefits of education for girls in rural Balochistan are only recently being recognized. The Mobile Female Teacher Training Unit is a project that was developed out of the realization that girls and women in rural areas deserve an education and that their role in rural development depends on their larger participation in the process.

[2] Saleem Shahid, 'Balochistan has highest female mortality rate in the world', *Dawn*, 9 September 2020.

[3] Muhammad Akbar, 'Shocking Conditions for Balochistan's Women', Diplomat, 29 March 2015.

The lives of many of the women in Pakistan, especially Balochistan and the NWFP, were often confined to the 'chadar and chardiwari', where the proper place for a woman was in a veil and within the four walls of her house. Patriarchy was strong in Pakistani society, leading to an imbalance in gender power relations. The seclusion and segregation of women isolated them and confined them to the household. This left little or no room for access to the wider society, thus, denying them the opportunity to play any role outside the home.[4]

While searching for a place to live, we went to the house of a respected Balochi political figure. While my husband was taken to engage with the men, I was taken to be with the women. They were privileged as they had travelled to Islamabad. But that seemed to be the end of their privilege. Their world was confined to the boundary walls of their house. I asked them about their personal shopping. They replied simply, without any rancour and with complete acceptance, 'The items are brought to us at home, even clothes.'

During the global coronavirus pandemic, we chafed about our confinement for a few weeks at a time. It seems impossible to believe that so many women spend lifetimes confined to their homes.

Islamabad presented a picture of a modern Pakistan to the casual observer. But women were invariably clubbed with other women, regardless of profession. Segregation of men and women was common even in diplomatic gatherings, partly perhaps because many houses had two small living rooms. At most diplomatic dinners, men and women would be seated separately; mixing of genders was not even attempted.

---

[4] T.S. Ali, S.S. Ali, S. Nadeem, et al. 'Perpetuation of gender discrimination in Pakistani society: Results from a scoping review and qualitative study conducted in three provinces of Pakistan', BMC Women's Health (2022).

Dinners and cocktails are part of the working life of a diplomat. One often picks up titbits of information which help in understanding a new place and society better. People often talk about politics or the prevailing economic situation or important local developments. That is why, despite being a virtual teetotaller, I attended every cocktail I could, nursing a glass of soda water with a slice of lemon thrown in. While cocktails allowed free mingling, segregation was the norm at dinners. Being a woman, especially one from the subcontinent, I often got a taste of gender-based segregation!

Women's social groups may not always have been professionally useful, but they were often a lot of fun. Working in a man's world, I missed the finer joys of womanhood. The conversation was not always about the house and children. There would often be other professional women in the group, even bankers or artists. Many of the women I met at these gatherings were smart and well educated and engaged in convivial conversation. There was often a lot of local gossip. While Pakistani men would be guarded in the presence of Indian diplomats, the women talked far more freely in my presence about powerful people in Pakistan. I learnt about the frailties and weaknesses of Pakistan's leaders and generals, both past and present. One lady described how her brother-in-law, a senior army officer, scolded her after she danced with the then army chief of Pakistan, who was the most powerful man in the country in those days. She laughingly narrated to the group how the general's weakness for attractive women was pointed out to her by her brother-in-law.

A few days later, as we discussed Pakistan's domestic situation in one of the early-morning meetings in the high commissioner's office, it struck me that my colleagues had no idea about the hidden aspects of the lives of people in power. I realized then the worth of my Pakistani women friends!

Diplomacy has traditionally been an almost exclusive male preserve. The tools employed by diplomats to practise their craft were developed by men for use by other men. Traditionally, diplomats would get a lot of work done sitting and drinking (alcohol) with each other. The image of a quintessential diplomat in people's minds in those days was a man with a glass in one hand and a cigar in the other.

With the entry of women in diplomacy, these traditional methods of practising the craft were no longer tenable for all. Women would often consume alcohol only in small quantities, even in Western societies. The preferred drink would often have been wine rather than harder versions of alcohol, like whiskey or cognac. Women in traditional Indian families did not consume alcohol at all. As a professional, I tried to sip alcohol, but my body would be in revolt at the first sip. Neither the love of my profession, nor the love of my country could induce me to go beyond a couple of sips of alcohol. With great effort, I could only manage to drink half a glass of wine. On one occasion, my husband joined in to help, so that I could carry out a conversation. This, though, was the only instance and was not totally successful.

In the male-dominated world of diplomacy, a considerable amount of work would be transacted on the golf course, where one could spend hours with one's interlocutors. While some women golfers did enjoy playing golf even in those days, I had neither talent nor time, and thus, no inclination for golf. As a mother of two small children and with a full-time profession, I was loath to spend long hours on the golf course.

It is also true that women are judged more readily, and one small failure tends to be blown out of proportion. Male officers tended to believe that the more substantive work should come to them, while their female colleagues should be left to handle housekeeping-related jobs. Such prejudices tend to get more acute when one is surrounded by a male chauvinistic society like that in Pakistan.

Thankfully, like most conservative societies in Asia, urban Pakistan had several women high achievers. Asma Jahangir and

Hina Jilani were without doubt among the best examples of empowered women in Pakistan. The two sisters were lawyers at the Supreme Court of Pakistan. They had set up Pakistan's first all-women legal aid practice. AGHS Legal Aid was the first free legal aid centre in Pakistan. The AGHS Legal Aid Cell in Lahore also ran a shelter for women, called Dastak (meaning 'knock'). Asma and Hina were among the co-founders of the Human Rights Commission of Pakistan. Both were passionate defenders of human rights, especially rights of women, persecuted minorities and children. They had set up the Women's Action Forum, a pressure group campaigning against Pakistan's discriminatory legislation. Both had endured threats (including death threats) from religious groups.

During our stay in Islamabad, their legal office and Dastak became front-page news when a young woman, Samia Sarwar, who had sought shelter at Dastak, was shot dead in Jilani's office by a guard accompanying Samia's mother. Samia had apparently been married against her will by her parents. She had two children. She had sought the help of Jahangir and Jilani in seeking a divorce from what she claimed was an abusive marriage. Samia's mother came with a gunman on the pretext of seeking reconciliation with her daughter. The gunman shot Samia dead. He also fired at Jilani, who managed to escape. Jahangir was then the United Nations Special Rapporteur on extrajudicial killings.[5]

Despite the public outrage, protests and media coverage, no one was punished. The Pakistani penal code of the day recognized[6] the

---

[5] Asma Jahangir was appointed as the United Nations Special Rapporteur on extrajudicial, arbitrary or summary executions in 1998 and as the UN Special Rapporteur on freedom of religion and belief in 2004.

[6] The First Ordinance of the Qisas and Diyat Law was promulgated by Pakistan's President Ghulam Ishaq Khan during the interim government of PM Ghulam Mustafa Jatoi, on 5 September 1990.

Islamic practices of Qisas (equal retribution) and Diyat (monetary compensation to kin of victims),[7] under which the Pakistani state does not press charges even for heinous crimes like murder if the next-of-kin of the victim accepts restitution or grants forgiveness to the culprit. As her Wali, or her first-ranking kin, Samia's father granted forgiveness to the assassin and his accomplice (Samia's mother). A resolution framed by Senator Iqbal Haider, of the PPP, was tabled in the house but was vehemently opposed by members of the Senate. The chairman of the Senate, Wasim Sajjad, ruled against a discussion about honour killings in the Upper House on 2 August 1999, prompting the Oxford University Students Union to pass a resolution against him.[8] Sajjad was a Rhodes Scholar and the Head of Rhodes Scholarship Selection Committee of Pakistan. He had also served as the minister for law and justice! This case became one of the most prominent examples of 'honour killing' in Pakistan and prompted multiple analyses of the misuse of Qisas and Diyat in Pakistan.

Even as scores of Muslim women in Pakistan became victims of 'honour killing' or 'honour revenge', the position of minority women seemed much worse. Girls as young as twelve to eighteen years of age from the Hindu, Christian and Sikh communities could be kidnapped, raped, forcibly converted to Islam and married

---

[7] Nikhat Sattar, 'Qisas & Diyat Laws', *Dawn*, 5 May 2023: In case after case of murder and severe bodily harm to innocent people, the perpetrators are often given a clean chit by Pakistan's courts. The accused, even more emboldened, returns to society with no remorse. Many are legislators—elected by the very same people they harmed.

[8] Ardeshir Cowasjee, 'Are we perverse?' *Dawn*, 16 February 2003 provides details: 'Once a Rhodes Scholar at Oxford University, on February 8, 2002, he was sternly censured by the Oxford University Student Union and a motion was passed against him unanimously condemning the irresponsible behaviour of former chairman of the Pakistan Senate, Mr Wasim Sajjad, for not allowing debate on "Honour Killing" on the 2nd August, 1999'.

to Muslim men, with almost no justice available to the victims or their families. Even when the cases were brought before courts, the victims were threatened and intimidated by their abductors to state that the conversion was of their own free will. Somehow, it was always young girls who seemed to 'convert' to Islam and marry much older Muslim men following their conversion!

A report by the South Asia Partnership Pakistan (SAP-PK), a volunteer network of participatory development-support organizations, stated that 'the percentage of forced conversion cases in Sindh during the last 15 years is equal to the number of such cases that happened from 1947 to 1987'.[9] SAP-PK released a report in collaboration with Aurat Foundation in July 2015 stating that at least 1000 girls are forcibly converted to Islam in Pakistan every year.[10] The report defined a forced conversion as when a person/persons use any sort of pressure, force, duress or threat—physical, emotional or psychological—to make another person adopt another religion.[11]

Forced conversions and marriages have remained a recurring problem in Pakistan. Even if the girls are minors, once they have been converted to Islam and married to Muslims, they cannot leave the marriage or disavow Islam, as that would be considered apostasy, and Islamic law and shariat don't allow it. Often, due to

---

[9] For details, see 'Forced Conversion of Religion', July 2015 report by South Asia Partnership Pakistan.

[10] Shahid Husain, '1,000 girls forcibly converted to Islam in Pakistan every year', News International, 15 July 2015, Also see Anwar Iqbal, '1000 minority girls forced in marriage every year: report', Dawn, 8 April 2014; Veengas, 'Bring back our girls: Pakistan's Hindus against forced conversions', Wire, 14 January 2017.

[11] Imtiaz Mugheri and Hafsa Chaudhry, 'Sindh assembly adopts bill against forced religious conversion', Dawn, 24 November 2016; See also 'Pakistan: Sindh Provincial Assembly Passes New Law Prohibiting Forced Religious Conversion', and 'Pakistan: Sindh Province Rejects Bill Against Forced Conversions', Library of Congress.

change of religion, the victims are not allowed to see their families. As a result, such victims gradually get separated from their families and are socially excluded. In some cases, forced conversion is exploited as a tool for human trafficking.[12] A part of the problem was that society in Pakistan was conflicted over crimes involving forced conversions, due to the 'sawab', or spiritual reward, that conversion of non-Muslims was believed to bring.

The problem was compounded by the Hudood Ordinances,[13] a series of discriminatory laws that were introduced as a part of the process of Islamization by Zia-ul-Haq. Promulgated in 1979, the Hudood Ordinances equated rape with adultery. A woman's testimony was not admitted to prove rape or adultery; instead, evidence is required of four adult Muslim males of good reputation about whom the court is satisfied that they meet the criteria of being credible witnesses, that they are truthful persons and abstain from major sins. Non-Muslims were also discriminated and could testify only if the victim was non-Muslim. Thus, it would mean that a Muslim man could not be punished for raping a Muslim woman in the presence of women or non-Muslim men, or even Muslim men, if the court determined that the Muslim men were not of 'good standing'.

By equating rape with adultery, when a charge of rape is brought, the burden of proof falls on the accusing women. However, as women's evidence is not accepted and four reliable, pious male Muslim witnesses are unlikely to be available, generally the charge can't be made to stick. As a result, the woman herself becomes accused of adultery. Thousands of women who claimed to be rape victims ended up languishing in jail.

---

[12] Forced Conversion of Religion, South Asia Partnership-Pakistan.

[13] See 'Women and religious minorities under the Hudood Laws in Pakistan', Asian Human Rights Commission; Maliha Zia Lari, 'Rape Laws in Pakistan: A History of Injustice, *Dawn*, 30 March 2014.

While honour killings, abductions and forced conversions of young girls from minority communities were depressing enough, the misuse of the infamous Blasphemy Laws was even more distressing. Introduced by the British colonial authorities, these laws were made much more severe under General Zia-ul-Haq between 1980 and 1986. It included a provision that applied to Ahmadis,[14] who were declared non-Muslims by the Second Amendment to the Constitution of Pakistan on 7 September 1974. Pakistani laws prohibit the Ahmadis from identifying themselves as Muslims, thus curtailing their freedom of religion.

The Blasphemy Laws targeted not just the Ahmadis and members of the minority community, especially Christians, but also Muslims. The law was often misused to settle personal scores. Justice was difficult in such cases as lawyers and judges would be targeted by right-wing extremists. Shortly after our arrival in Islamabad, Justice Arif Iqbal Hussain Bhatti, a judge of the Lahore High Court, was murdered on 17 October 1997. He had acquitted two Christian men of blasphemy charges in a judgment along with another judge; the men were accused of having written the blasphemous material in Arabic, a language they did not know. About a year later, the police arrested Sher Khan, who confessed to having killed Justice Bhatti for having acquitted the two blasphemy accused persons. Khan mysteriously disappeared from police custody.[15]

---

[14] An Islamic sect founded by Mirza Ghulam Ahmad, Islamic religious figure from Qadian in India, who proclaimed himself the promised Messiah, the Mahdi. This is regarded as heretic and non-Islamic as Prophet Muhammad is considered the last Prophet by the Muslims. Ahmadis believe Prophet Muhammad to be the final law-bearing prophet but teach the continuity of prophethood.

[15] 'Timeline: Accused under the Blasphemy Law', *Dawn*, 19 September 2012.

Even as these reports anguished us deeply, we were conscious of the rising tide of terrorism emanating from around us. On 7 August 1998, over a year into our stay in Islamabad, the world was shaken by the near simultaneous bombing outside the embassies of the US in Nairobi, Kenya and Dar es Salam, Tanzania. Over 200 people were killed, including twelve Americans, while over 4500 were reported wounded. Both bombings were carried out by explosive-laden trucks. These attacks brought Osama bin Laden, Ayman al-Zawahiri and the Al-Qaeda,[16] to world attention. Bin Laden was placed on the list of ten most-wanted fugitives by the Federal Bureau of Investigation.

Within two weeks of these attacks, on 20 August, US President Bill Clinton ordered retaliatory cruise missile strikes on Al-Qaeda bases in the Khost Province[17] of Afghanistan (and the Al-Shifa pharmaceutical factory in Khartoum, Sudan[18]). Codenamed 'Operation Infinite Reach', the cruise missiles were launched from ships in the Persian Gulf and targeted six terrorism-related sites near Khost. Statements in the US underlined the link between the targets and those responsible for the 7 August bombings of two US embassies in East Africa and pointed to Bin Laden's link to the facilities attacked.

The missile strikes in Khost on Al-Qaeda's training camps were aimed at pre-empting more attacks. It was described as

---

[16] United Nations Security Council resolution 1267 adopted unanimously on 15 October 1999 designated Osama bin Laden and associates as terrorists and established a sanctions regime covering individuals and entities associated with Al-Qaeda, and/or the Taliban wherever located. The Al-Qaeda was founded by bin Laden and others in 1988 and is a multinational network of militant and extremist Sunni Jihadists. Bin Laden was killed in his house in Abbottabad just 1.3 km (3⁄4 mi) southwest of the Pakistan Military Academy on 2 May 2011.

[17] One of the thirty-four provinces of Afghanistan, bordered by Pakistan's North Waziristan on the south and Kurram on the north.

[18] The attack on Al-Shifa factory became controversial.

'one of the most active terrorist bases in the world . . . operated by groups affiliated with Osama bin Laden'.[19] Bin Laden was not present at the time of the attack which only damaged the installations and inflicted an uncertain number of casualties. The Afghan Islamic Press, an Afghan news service set up in 1982 in Peshawar, reported that at least fifteen people were killed by the missile strike in Afghanistan. Pakistani News Agency, News Network International (NNI) quoted the HuM,[20] as saying that the strike killed five of its Pakistani fighters, who were training to fight in India.

The missiles fired at Khost flew over unspecified parts of Pakistan. Apparently, no prior information was given, nor was overflight permission asked from the Pakistani authorities. The US chargé d'affaires was summoned to the Pakistan Ministry of Foreign Affairs to protest the presumed airspace violations during these strikes.[21]

Angry reactions, including violence, were expected on the streets of Pakistan. Retaliation against US forces and US interests in the region was anticipated. US had warned its non-Muslim foreign aid workers to leave Afghanistan a day before the attack citing 'credible threats' and evacuated all but essential embassy staff in Pakistan.

All the schoolgoing children from our High Commission, including our two sons, were studying at the American School in Islamabad. The school authorities called an emergency meeting of representatives of diplomatic missions and others to review the security scenario. I also went to the meeting. For the first

---

[19] Barton Gellman and Dana Priest, 'U.S. Strikes Terrorist-Linked Sites in Afghanistan, Factory in Sudan', *Washington Post*, 21 August 1998.

[20] Based in Pakistan (also Harkat-ul-Jihad-al-Islami and Harkat-ul-Ansar), a listed terrorist group, primarily targeting Jammu and Kashmir.

[21] 'Pakistan lodges protest over U.S. missile strikes', CNN, 21 August 1998.

time, I noticed the remote location of the school, the long drive, through several isolated patches and the unending open fields opposite the school. I worried about the school being attacked by a lone ranger, using a shoulder-fired missile from the safe distance of the vast open fields. Then, someone told me about a past kidnapping where the victim was taken to Afghanistan, adding to my anxiety.

I was initially relieved when the school authorities decided to close the school in the aftermath of the missile attacks on Khost. However, we soon started worrying about the children's education in the absence of the American School. The families of the US embassy staff had already been moved out of Pakistan, but there was no such decision by the Indian government. There was also no indication of when or if the school would restart. We, therefore, started looking at local schools where we could send the Indian children.

As all the children were affected, I visited a few Pakistani schools to try and include them on the High Commission's panel of approved schools. Unfortunately, nothing seemed to work out. One school was interested to be included in the High Commission's panel. Its primary section was run from a private house just across the street from our house. They asked for a couple of days to give a final answer. Two days later they apologized, saying that the husbands of some of their teachers were employed in the (nuclear and missile) plants in Kahuta. They conveyed frankly that they had been denied clearance by the intelligence agencies.

In this situation, we thought of sending the children to India for schooling. I made a visit to Delhi on courier duty and tried to approach the Vasant Valley School in Vasant Kunj, New Delhi, but did not get very far with that. It was a relief when the American School decided to start some limited teaching with reduced hours and no school bus. In the absence of many of the

American teachers who had themselves been evacuated, this was more than we could expect. An official van from the Mission was deputed to take the children to school and back. Given the limited seating, the little ones would sit in the laps of the older children. We instructed the van to change its route randomly for additional security. Fortunately, there was no untoward incident.

During this period, I went to a local bookshop one day and saw giant-sized posters of Bin Laden being sold openly at the most prominent bookshop in the heart of Islamabad. The poster identified US, Israel and India as enemies and prominently highlighted the Al-Qaeda's ambition to fly 'the green flag of Islam' over India's Red Fort! We were already agitated that extremist organizations could openly raise funds in Pakistan by fanning hatred for India in the name of the so-called 'Kashmir cause'. The Al-Qaeda poster added another red flag to our persistent security challenges.

With these turbulent currents around us, our life went on with its mundane rhythm. When the children stayed home, we worried that they had no friends to play with, affecting their social development. But when we sent them out to play with the children in the neighbourhood, they invariably returned when an 'India versus Pakistan' debate with the Pakistani children turned acrimonious.

When they were on their own, including at school, the children felt the need to stand up for their country. The Pakistani class teacher of our younger son complained to us at a parent–teacher meet about his propensity to get into arguments with other children over India. As parents, we overlooked this, as it would have been a difficult position for the eight-year-old who felt he needed to show courage and stand up to his classmates for the sake of his country. We felt that we had to give him space so long as his quarrels were settled without getting into physical fights.

A few years later, our younger son was confined to the house during his summer vacation in Delhi with his legs in plaster; he was injured in a fall from a mountain side during a school trip. To keep him occupied, I gave him a writing assignment about his days as a student in a school in Pakistan. He wrote about his class teacher complaining to his parents and his arguments in class when India was criticized. India–Pakistan cricket matches became the fiercest debating issues between the few Indian children and their Pakistani classmates. His innocent perspective appealed to the then editor of the online edition of *Outlook* weekly magazine and the write-up appeared as the lead story in the online edition.[22] It was the week that the Delhi–Lahore bus service was resumed, which had been discontinued following the terror attack by Pakistan-based terrorists on the Indian Parliament.

Given the many pressures and demands of a posting in Islamabad, I had to juggle many balls. Early mornings on weekends, the children would wake us up as it was time to take them for their baseball games at the American Club. It was also the time I had to read the Friday editions of the weekly newspapers that were so important to keep track of developments in the country. My husband shared the responsibility, but I took them for their activities on several days. From reading the papers while sitting on the stands, to dictating reports while sponging a child in high fever or helping the kids with their homework and solving maths problems on the phone while on official tour, we found innovative ways to cope. Perhaps, not unlike other working couples elsewhere.

It was not always smooth sailing though. I often forgot Ghanashyam's official contacts who had been to our home for dinner. Every time I mistakenly extended my hand to introduce

---

[22] Aniket Ghanashyam, 'An Indian Student in Pakistan', *Outlook*, 10 July 2003.

myself to a strange-looking man, he would gently nudge me with his elbow to remind me, and then we would try and cover up as diplomatically as possible!

15

Understanding Pakistan

'You are free; you are free to go to your temples, you are free to go to your mosques or to any other place of worship in this State of Pakistan. You may belong to any religion or caste or creed—that has nothing to do with the business of the State . . .' said Mohammed Ali Jinnah, the founding father of Pakistan, in his speech to the Constituent Assembly of Pakistan on 11 August 1947. After successfully creating a separate state for the Muslims of India, an essentially non-secular construct, Jinnah wanted, not an Islamic State, but a modern and secular Pakistan.

Having tilled the ground for Pakistan's creation with slogans like, '*Pakistan ka matlab kya? La Ilaha Illa Allah*' (What does Pakistan mean? There is no God but Allah), this 'secular vision' never had a future. There was an expectation in Pakistan that as a state for Muslims, Pakistan would have a pre-eminent place for Islam and would become an Islamic State.

Jinnah's own statements, both before and after Partition, created ambiguity about what he really wanted. Did he want a

Pakistan governed by the Sharia with protection for its minorities, perhaps in return for protection for the minority Muslims left behind in India?[1] Or was he committed to the secular vision that seems to emerge from his famous statement of 11 August 1947? Soon after the 11 August statement, during an address to Karachi Bar Association on 25 January 1948, Jinnah seemed to favour a Constitution of Pakistan based on the Sharia, dismissing secularist assertions as deliberate and mischievous propaganda. He said that Islamic principles remained 'as applicable to life as they were 1,300 years ago'.

It did not take long for Islam to become the state religion of Pakistan after Jinnah's death. The Objectives Resolution was passed on 12 March 1949, under Pakistan's first prime minister, Nawabzada Liaquat Ali Khan, overriding the concerns and objections of minority members of the Constituent Assembly. The Objectives Resolution[2] forms the preamble for the constitution of 1956, 1962 and 1973 and became part of Pakistan's Constitution of 1973.

This Objectives Resolution set the stage for minoritization of Ahmadis, Shias, Hindus, Sikhs and Christians. Once territory was divided based on belief, certain members of the population became 'minorities'. Over time, they came to be treated as 'strangers in their own house', the outsiders within. It was not

---

[1] Ishtiaq Ahmed in *Jinnah: His Successes, Failures and Role in History*, questions Jinnah's inherent secularity, stating that in reality, the discourse 'was meant to prevent the exodus (from India) of millions of Muslims towards Pakistan'. Jinnah believed, according to Ahmed, that such an inflow of Muslim refugees would further strain the already overstretched resources of Pakistan. Review by Amit Cowshish, Wire, 27 March 2021 titled, 'Review: A Book That Busts Many Myths Surrounding Jinnah'.

[2] It contained the basic principles of the Islamic political system and Western democracy and starts with 'Whereas sovereignty over the entire universe belongs to Allah Almighty alone.'

long before certain sections of the ruling classes, brandishing a specific version of religion, came to use the idea of 'majority rule' to attain power. In post-Partition Pakistan, majority rule came to mean rule of the religious majority.[3] Democracy, thus, became hostage to religion and it was only logical that the name of the country changed from Republic of Pakistan to Islamic Republic of Pakistan, and non-Muslims were denied the right to be head of state or government.[4]

Confronted with a deteriorating economy and inadequate governance, it was not long before Pakistan tumbled into martial law and military rule under Field Marshal Muhammad Ayub Khan, eleven years into its existence as a nation, in 1958.

Ayub Khan (1958–69) tried to distance himself publicly from religious elements but wasn't above using religion for political expediency. He used the Islami Jamiat-e-Talaba, the student wing of Jamaat Islami, in the civil war with Awami League in East Pakistan; and invited Jamaat-e-Islami's founder, Sayyid Abul Ala al-Mawdudi, to speak on the radio in favour of 'jihad' when faced with a war against India in 1965.[5] It was in his regime that the 1962 constitution provided for the president of Pakistan to be a Muslim. He established the Advisory Council of Islamic Ideology and the Islamic Research Institute to assist the

---

[3] Rubina Saigol, 'Strangers in the House', *Herald*, 24 May 2013.

[4] In his book, *Jinnah: His Successes, Failures and Role in History*, Ishtiaq Ahmed argues that the narrative popular in Pakistan that the March 1949 Objectives Resolution adopted by Pakistan's Constituent Assembly, which proclaimed that the country's constitution would be modelled on the ideology of the Islamic faith was not a betrayal of Jinnah's vision, and was, in fact, 'a manifestation of the overwhelming majority view that Jinnah promised them a Pakistan which would embody Islamic principles in letter and spirit'.

[5] Aarish Ullah Khan, 'The Terrorist Threat and the Policy Response in Pakistan', SIPRI Policy Paper No. 11, Stockholm International Peace Research Institute, September 2005.

government in reconciling all legislation with the tenets of the Quran and the sunnah.

Zulfikar Ali Bhutto became prime minister of (west) Pakistan, following the creation of Bangladesh in 1971. It was during his time that a more Islamic constitution of 1973 came to being. He also conceded to the demand of the Islamists to declare Ahmadis as non-Muslims. Bhutto changed the name of Red Cross to Red Crescent, established a ministry of religious affairs and adopted Islamic measures like banning of alcohol and gambling, and closing casinos and nightclubs.

General Zia-ul-Haq provided state patronage to religious bodies leading to development of Islamism as an instrument of policy. Zia deposed Bhutto in a military coup, imposed martial law in 1977 and stayed in power (as President from September 1978) until his death in 1988. Militant religious organizations in Pakistan involved in terrorism, originated in the period after 1979.[6] While General Zia's personal convictions were partially responsible for the growth of Islamism, the Soviet invasion of Afghanistan in 1979 and the Iranian revolution created the complementary foil for the growth of radicalization under Zia.

Following the 1979–88 Afghanistan War, proponents of jihad had a free run under Zia's government. Many madrassas came up in Pakistan. There is no reliable statistics for the number of madrassas as many are unregistered or operate illegally. It is estimated that of the 3906 registered madrasas in 1995, as many as 2010 had been established after 1979. In 1947, only 189 madrassas operated in Pakistan. This number had risen to an estimate of over 40,000 in 2008, with at least eighty of them functioning in Islamabad.[7] The 2017–18 Pakistan Education Statistics survey reported a

---

[6] Ibid.
[7] Kamila Hyat, 'No room for doubt and division', News International, 25 September 2008.

total of 31,115 madrassas operating in the country, with a total enrolment of 4.099 million and employing 0.179 million teachers,[8] while an International Forum for Rights and Security report estimated between 32,000 and 72,000 madrassas with around 2.5 million students.[9]

As an institution, the madrassa could be seen as a harmless avenue for educating the poor. However, they became the essential source of manpower for 'jihadist' activities, providing trained and motivated foot soldiers for the war against communism in Afghanistan.

In a study, columnist Huma Yusuf says that major madrassas were key to incubating various extremist organizations.

> The Jamia Uloom Islamia in Binori Town has long supplied Deobandi militants to various jihadi organisations and helped establish groups such as the Harkat-ul-Mujahideen and the Jaish-e-Mohammad . . . madrassas continue to disseminate sectarian and extremist ideologies through unreformed curricula ... (they) house members of banned militant groups and give them opportunities to generate funds, approach potential recruits, and expand their network of freelance militants. Madrassas are particularly important for militant fundraising because there is no monitoring of the funds that flow through religious schools . . . Madrassas also offer facilities to produce and distribute jihadi and sectarian publications, CDs, DVDs, and other material. As such, they are largely responsible for the spread of extremist ideologies

[8] Izza Tahir, 'Decolonizing Madrassa Reform in Pakistan', University of Toronto, *Current Issues in Comparative Education (CICE)*, Vol. 24, No. 1, Winter 2022, based on NEMIS et al., 2021.

[9] 'Female radicalization rising in Pakistan: Report', ANI, April 2022.

across the city (Karachi), including . . . among university students.[10]

After the withdrawal of Soviet forces from Afghanistan, foreign interest and resources supporting the war against the Soviet Union disappeared. Pakistan continued to support, recruit and train religious radicals for operating in Kashmir and to secure its 'strategic interests' in Afghanistan. Thus, began Pakistan's quest for the so-called 'strategic depth' in Afghanistan, aimed at facilitating the continuation of insurgency in Kashmir, as well as providing defence against aggression from India. The quest for 'strategic depth' underpinned Pakistan's support to the Taliban in 1994. The Afghan Taliban was itself a creation of the ISI, and a de facto Pakistan proxy by the time it took over Kabul in 1996. In 1999, Benazir Bhutto's Minister of Interior, Naseerullah Babar, admitted it quite explicitly, pronouncing, 'We created the Taliban.'[11]

Pakistan began infiltrating recently unemployed Afghan Mujahideen and Pakistani volunteers from terrorist groups like LeT, JeM and LeJ into Kashmir. This converted a secular political agitation in Kashmir into a religious war. Kashmiris in large numbers were also exfiltrated to Pakistan and Afghanistan for training in arms and guerrilla warfare. The pan-Islamic bonds created between them and the Afghan Mujahideen lent a new dimension to militancy in Kashmir. As part of Pakistan's strategy, the insurgency in Kashmir was taken over by Islamist radicals and foreign mercenaries. Though there was no clear victory for Pakistan in Kashmir, it did succeed in injecting

---

[10] Huma Yusuf, 'Conflict Dynamics in Karachi', United States Institute of Peace, 2012.

[11] 'Pakistan Army and Terrorism; an unholy alliance', an August 2017 study paper by European Foundation for South Asian Studies, EFSAS.

a communal ideology and converting a political issue into a religious one. This destroyed the social fabric of Kashmir and the political and social cohesion between diverse ethnic and religious subgroups that once existed in Jammu and Kashmir.[12] This religious schism eventually forced the Kashmiri Pandits to abandon their homes and hearth, becoming refugees in their own land.

The chickens soon came home to roost in Pakistan. While it succeeded in creating a religious divide in Jammu and Kashmir, its 'jihadi' protégée soon realized that efforts were needed to create an idyllic Islamic utopia in their own homeland. Radical entities started turning their attention inwards as well. Their enemies were no longer restricted to Indians and Kashmiri Hindus. At home in Pakistan, Shias, Ahmadis, Sufis, Christians and minorities became the enemies.

During our stay in Islamabad, the sectarian divide was out in the open. Zia's pro-Sunni agenda had antagonized the Shias, at a time when the (Shiite) Islamic Revolution in Iran had bolstered the morale of the Shias. Frequent killings of both Sunnis and Shias were reported in the media on a regular basis. Pakistan's largest city, Karachi, and the province of Punjab seemed most affected by the relentless sectarian killings. Mutual killings among Barelvi and Deobandi Sunnis also became a regular feature.

Between early February 1997 to February 1998, more than 300 people were killed in religiously motivated violence. Eight Iranians were killed in obviously religiously motivated killings in different incidents in Pakistan. The dead included five Iranian Air Force technicians in the garrison city of Rawalpindi, adjacent to Islamabad and an Iranian diplomat at the Iranian cultural centre

---

[12] Ibid.

in Multan, in eastern Punjab.[13] It was widely believed that the Arab Iranian rivalry post the Iran–Iraq war was manifested in the Sunni–Shia hostility in Pakistan.

The nefarious activities of sectarian and radical Islamic groups have, over the years, extended to criminal acts within Pakistan. Dacoities, bank robberies, kidnappings for ransom and extortion became a part of the militant groups' toolkit.[14] The Tehrik-e-Taliban Pakistan has long generated vital financing for its activities from Karachi through bank robberies.[15] Fourteen major bank heists occurred in Karachi in 2009 and twenty in 2010.[16] More than a hundred kidnappings for ransom took place in Karachi in 2010[17] and eighty-nine traders and industrialists were kidnapped between January and October 2011.[18]

The radical Islamic groups in Pakistan seem committed to waging a 'holy war' against everything that they see as un-Islamic. Unseating governments, terrorising and killing Muslims and non-Muslim minorities are considered justifiable in the cause of creating an Islamic Caliphate. Pakistan is a nuclear state that faces a brutal insurgency within, posing a threat to peace and

---

[13] 'Issue Paper: Pakistan Sectarian Violence July 1999', Immigration and Refugee Board of Canada.

[14] Details available in Aarish Ullah Khan, 'The Terrorist Threat and the Policy Response in Pakistan', SIPRI Policy Paper No. 11, Stockholm International Peace Research Institute, September 2005.

[15] Huma Yusuf, 'Conflict Dynamics in Karachi', United States Institute of Peace, 2012.

[16] Citizens–Police Liaison Committee (CPLC), a public–private initiative to fight urban crime; quoted by Huma Yusuf.

[17] Salman Siddiqui, 'Kidnapping for Ransom Cases Hit 20-Year High', *Express Tribune*, 4 November 2010, http://tribune.com.pk/story/72260/kidnapping-for-ransom-cases-hit-20-year-high/, quoted by Huma Yusuf.

[18] '89 Abducted during 2011 in Karachi', *Nation*, 15 October 2011; quoted by Huma Yusuf.

security within Pakistan and creating a wall between Pakistan and development of any kind.[19]

Unsuccessful efforts have been made by Pakistan to contain the growing menace of religious extremism, but the tentacles of extreme radical groups have only gone deeper into the Pakistani society as the efforts have been half-hearted and, thus, doomed to fail. 'When it comes to the jihadis involved in Kashmir, the policy level approach seems, at best, divided and, at worst, hesitant.'[20] Others bemoan the 'selective approach of security agencies towards counterterrorism', which has enabled these groups to develop into 'Frankenstein's Monsters for both people and the state', making the goal of 'peace in Pakistan' or mellowing down of 'Pakistan-sponsored terrorism' in its neighbourhood a distant dream. This is so, as many in the Pakistan Army and ISI believe that terrorism still has an external utility in Afghanistan, India and 'Indian Administered Jammu & Kashmir'.[21]

The militant Islamic groups have had an adverse impact on the economy of Pakistan. In the past, Pakistan provided the safest route for foreign fighters to enter Afghanistan. Some of these foreign groups decided to stay back and pursue their own agendas against economic targets in Pakistan. Foreign investments and projects were not spared. A negative economic environment has been created by frequent incidents of terrorist attacks within Pakistan and the criminal activities of the radical Islamic groups. This negative environment, especially the near impunity and

---

[19] See 'Pakistan Army and Terrorism; an unholy alliance', an August 2017 study paper by European Foundation for South Asian Studies, EFSAS.

[20] Aarish Ullah Khan, 'The Terrorist Threat and the Policy Response in Pakistan' SIPRI Policy Paper No. 11, Stockholm International Peace Research Institute.

[21] 'Pakistan Army and Terrorism; an unholy alliance', an August 2017 study paper by European Foundation for South Asian Studies, EFSAS.

freedom of operation available to the radical groups, has become a major impediment to attracting investment.

One of the bottlenecks in controlling the growth of radical Islam is that the Pakistan Army and ISI continue distinguishing between 'bad' terrorists (those who target Pakistani Security Forces) and 'good' terrorists (those who advance its strategic objectives vis-á-vis Afghanistan and India especially Jammu and Kashmir). As former US Secretary of State, Hillary Clinton said, 'You can't keep snakes in your backyard and expect them to only bite your neighbour.'[22]

People in Pakistan often tend to justify the growing radicalisation in the name of 'Kashmir', believing that the cost of radicalization is a necessary concomitant to its support for Kashmir. The peril caused to Pakistan's polity and society by these extremist 'jihadi' outfits is largely ignored. Pakistan's obsession with *Kashmir banega Pakistan* (Kashmir will become Pakistan) is self-destructive.

Pakistan's claim on Kashmir is often based on the story of the acronym supposedly coined by a Muslim student in Cambridge, Choudhary Rehmat Ali. It is said that in the 1930s, Rehmat Ali expressed the desire for a separate national status for a new entity consisting of Punjab, Afghanistan, Kashmir, Sindh and Balochistan.

Not everyone accepts this lore. Rehmat Ali's desire was dismissed as a student's dream by Muslim leaders and even the Muslim League. It seems far-fetched as the name 'Pakistan' has no place for Bengal (for East Pakistan inhabited by Bengalis) that became a part of Pakistan, though Kashmir, an independent princely state at the time, was included.

Another explanation is that the name 'Pakistan' was coined by one Khawaja Abdur Rehman when he read a British journal on

---

[22] Ibid.

Central Asia and came upon a map that showed 'Karakalpakstan' as a new autonomous region in Uzbekistan under Stalin. The map was printed in such a way that the book's spine separated 'Karakal' and 'Pakstan'. An 'i' was introduced in the Urdu version to create the name 'Pakistan'.

'Pakistan' means 'Land of the Pure', deriving from 'Pak' (pure) and 'stan' (land or place, from the Sanskrit word 'sthan'). The names of some other nations in the region, such as Afghanistan, Uzbekistan or Kazakhstan, lend credence to this origin of its name.

Pakistan's claim on Kashmir is sometimes made on the ground that Kashmir is the origin of all the rivers flowing through Pakistan. 'Kashmir is the source of the rivers that feed the Indus Valley. Water is an existential issue. Control over this life source cannot be legally surrendered to India.'[23] Such a claim is outlandish, if not ridiculous, and would make national boundaries irrelevant! If the source of river water determined boundaries, India would have a claim on Nepal and China, while Bangladesh would have a claim on territories of all three countries.

The basis for Pakistan's claim over 'Kashmir' and its devotion to the 'Kashmir cause', thus, remains an enigma. At the time of India's independence, the erstwhile princely states could join either India or Pakistan or remain independent. The ruler of Kashmir, Maharaja Hari Singh (a Hindu) did not wish to join either country. In violation of a Standstill Agreement that Pakistan had signed with the Maharaja, it sent raiders, including military forces, disguised as tribals into Kashmir. The Maharaja approached India for help and signed the Instrument of Accession, acceding to India on 26 October 1947. The Maharaja's offer of accession to India was supported by the National Conference, a predominantly Muslim non-communal political organization. The Instrument

---

[23] Munir Akram, ' "K" is for Kashmir', *Dawn*, 20 August 2017.

of Accession was accepted by the British governor general of India on 27 October 1947, following which, Jammu and Kashmir became an integral part of India. Indian troops landed in Kashmir following this and prevented the fall of Kashmir to the Pakistani raiders and regulars.

India approached the UN Security Council (UNSC) to get Pakistan to vacate its aggression in Kashmir. The UNSC set up a UN Commission for India and Pakistan. UN Security Council Resolution[24] 47 (1948) of 21 April 1948 asked Pakistan 'To secure the withdrawal from the State of Jammu and Kashmir of tribesmen and Pakistani nationals not normally resident therein who have entered the State for the purpose of fighting, and to prevent any intrusion into the State of such elements and any furnishing of material aid to those fighting in the State . . .' This was the first step to be completed before holding a plebiscite in Kashmir. Most Pakistanis who support the 'Kashmir cause' and justify support for insurgency in Kashmir citing UN resolutions, do so without having read the resolutions.

Much can be said about the nexus between the Pakistan Army, the ISI and terrorist groups. 'Pakistan has become a sponsor of terrorism and an epicentre of terror . . . An array of terrorist groups in Pakistan, Afghanistan and "Indian Administered Jammu and Kashmir" (J&K) are supported by Pakistan; albeit myopically. The very same groups are allied with the terrorist groups that the Pakistani State is fighting. In addition, many of the extremist groups sponsored by Pakistan are allied with Al Qaeda.'[25]

---

[24] The UN resolution (UNCIP resolutions) of 21 April 1948 is clear that intruders needed to vacate Jammu and Kashmir to create the conditions for holding a plebiscite.

[25] 'Pakistan Army and Terrorism; an unholy alliance', an August 2017 study paper by European Foundation for South Asian Studies, EFSAS.

Why does Pakistan continue its self-destructive support to radical Islamists to create mayhem in Kashmir when its claim over the territory is without justification? Most governments would have tried to introduce radical reforms in the face of the damage the futile pursuit continues to cause to the nation's society, polity and economy.

Some analysts believe that Pakistan feels a 'perceived existential threat from India'. Others say that it continues to send militants across the LoC 'to keep them occupied in the neighbouring territory' to avoid the risk 'of these Kashmir-specific terrorist groups finding their way back into the land of their sponsor'.[26]

The underlying reason is to be found, perhaps, in the special position that the Pakistan military occupies in the country. The military has been a major influence in shaping the country's politics. No prime minister of Pakistan has ever completed a full five-year term.[27] Forcible removals by the army either through military coups or by pulling the strings are often cited by experts as the bane of Pakistan's democracy.

Pakistan's first military coup happened as early as 1958, when General Ayub Khan seized power from President Iskander Mirza, who was exiled. Mirza had earlier abrogated the Constitution and appointed Ayub as chief martial law administrator. Ayub stayed in office till 1969, appointing General Yahya Khan as his successor. Yahya Khan resigned only in 1971 after the creation of Bangladesh and losing the 1971 War to India. Zulfikar Ali Bhutto was handed over the presidency and became prime minister after the 1973 constitution was passed.

---

[26] Ibid.

[27] See 'No Pakistani PM has completed a full term in office', Al Jazeera, 9 April 2022, for details.

Bhutto did not last long. He won the elections in March 1977, but was deposed by General Zia-ul-Haq in July of the same year. General Zia put Bhutto under house arrest, imposed martial law across Pakistan, dissolved the National Assembly and all provincial assemblies, and had the Constitution of Pakistan suspended. He postponed elections indefinitely and banned political parties. Bhutto was imprisoned, then hanged on 4 April 1979.

General Zia held the long-promised elections in 1985 and invited Muhammad Khan Junejo to form the government as the prime minister. Zia, himself was sworn in as President for a five-year term. Junejo was removed from power in 1988[28] using the controversial Eighth Amendment[29] on grounds of breakdown of law and order. Zia continued as President until his death in a plane crash.

Power then rotated between Nawaz Sharif and Benazir Bhutto, with allegations of ISI meddling. Sharif returned to power for a second non-consecutive term in February 1997 but was deposed within less than three years by his Army Chief General Pervez Musharraf through a military coup in October

---

[28] See Richard M. Weintraub 'Premier Dismissed in Pakistan', *Washington Post*, 30 May 1988.

[29] The Eighth Amendment to the Constitution of Pakistan strengthened the authority of the President, granting additional powers to dismiss the elected prime minister's government. It was drafted and later enforced by the government of General Zia-ul-Haq. The controversial Article 58 (2) (b) states:

'...... the President may also dissolve the National Assembly in his discretion where, in his opinion,

a situation has arisen in which the Government of the Federation cannot be carried on in accordance with the provisions of the Constitution and an appeal to the electorate is necessary.'

In 2010, the Eighteenth amendment reduced presidential powers, returning the government to a parliamentary republic.

1999. Musharraf became President in June 2001, subsequently winning a referendum in April 2002 which extended his rule for five more years. Musharraf finally resigned in 2008 and Asif Ali Zardari became the new President.

In Pakistan, the civilian authority must constantly look over its shoulders as the military and its agencies cast an overarching shadow over the civilian bodies. Any meaningful reform in Pakistan depends on the support of the army and the ISI. The constant undermining of the civilian authority by the army is the biggest challenge for meaningful reform. Pakistan's neighbourhood policy, especially its relations with India and Afghanistan, is a hostage of the army's stranglehold over the civilian authorities.

It is, thus, a vicious cycle that has put Pakistan on a slippery downward slope. The vice-like grip that the army has over vital policy makes it impossible for any civilian government to take on the militant Islamic entities; presuming that the civilian government itself desires such reform! Meanwhile, Pakistan continues its perilous journey to economic disaster.

In 2023, Pakistan faced economic disaster yet again. External assistance may help it tide over the immediate crisis, but there are no visible benefactors who could bring about a miraculous turnaround of the economy itself.

Pakistan's currency fell to its lowest ever against the US dollar in early 2023 following a steady downward spiral. Wheat has been in short supply as large swathes of agricultural land ravaged by floods limp towards recovery. Long power outages across the country could become worse as electricity companies struggle to keep power generation units running with rising cost of diesel, the import of which is precariously dependent on Pakistan's fast depleting forex reserves. Electricity bills are beyond most middle-class families and the government lacks resources to subsidize them. Macroeconomic risks are also cause for worry due to high current account deficit, high public debt and lower demand from its traditional export markets amid subdued global growth.[30]

Pakistan is no stranger to economic crisis. Until the 1980s, Pakistan had GDP growth rates higher than that of India and South Asia. That has not been the case for a very long time. The growth potential of Pakistan's economy has diminished considerably over the last decades. Pakistan has repeatedly reached out to IMF for financial assistance and approached the IMF twenty-three times[31] in seventy-five years by early 2023.

Pakistan is unable to generate the revenues required to sustain its imports. Its consumption-led, import-intensive growth model is an unsustainable economic model.[32] Unable to balance its expenditure with revenues, it has become aid-dependent and is trapped in a vicious cycle of perpetual borrowing. Repeated IMF borrowing only adds to its overall indebtedness. The problem is enhanced as Pakistan has very low tax collections as few people pay taxes: It has one of the lowest tax-to-GDP ratios in the world.

Pakistan has long benefited from its strategic location. Being on the Indian Ocean, sharing borders with both Iran and Afghanistan, it is considered a valuable doorway to Central Asia. For several decades, it served as the entry point for Afghanistan, first for the mujahideen's operations against the erstwhile Soviet Union, then against the Taliban following the terrorist attacks in the US on 11 September 2001 (9/11). Pakistan was a vital transit

---

[30] 'Pakistan's Economy Slows Down While Inflation Rises Amid Catastrophic Floods', World Bank's Press Release, 6 October 2022.

[31] 'Tough love: Pak has gone to IMF for bailouts 23 times in 75 years', *Economic Times,* 26 February 2023.

[32] Amol Agrawal, 'MC Explains | Pakistan's economy, which once outgrew India's, now sinks. What went wrong?' MoneyControl, 11 February 2023.

point during the war in Afghanistan by the coalition forces under the NATO-led UN-mandated International Security Assistance Force (ISAF)[33] and for the Resolute Support Mission (RSM).[34] Over the years, Western donors have been attracted by these factors, and needed Pakistan as a transit point for operations in Afghanistan.

These advantages have diminished over the years, as Afghanistan could not be developed as a route for transhipment of Central Asian oil and gas. After the US withdrawal from Afghanistan, the value of Pakistan's location eroded further. Its rent-seeking ability has been reduced by its increasing closeness with China (its biggest debtor) that faces post-Covid-19 strains on the economy. Increasing Chinese assertiveness has increased competition rather than cooperation with most Western and Southeast Asian countries.

Pakistan is, thus, in a difficult spot. Without any meaningful reforms, it would continue to remain trapped in a debt cycle. Reform looks difficult in the face of the military's stranglehold.

---

[33] NATO allies went into Afghanistan in 2001. From August 2003, NATO led the UN-mandated ISAF that aimed to create the conditions whereby the Afghan government could exercise its authority throughout the country and build the capacity of the Afghan national security forces, including in the fight against international terrorism. ISAF was completed in December 2014 when the Afghan National Defence and Security Forces assumed full responsibility for security across the country; 'NATO and Afghanistan', www.nato.int.topics_8189.

[34] In January 2015, NATO launched the Resolute Support Mission (RSM) to train, advise and assist Afghan Security forces and institutions to fight terrorism and secure their country. Following the completion of the withdrawal of all RSM forces in August 2021, the Mission was terminated in early September 2021, following which NATO suspended all support to Afghanistan. 'NATO and Afghanistan', www.nato.int. topics_8189.

The road ahead may well be one of mounting debt and deteriorating economy.

With an economy in the doldrums, an increasing tussle between the army and the civilians, and a governance deficit, the support base of the extremists can only increase, eroding Pakistan's ability to control terrorist groups.

Given the dominant role of the military and its agencies in Pakistan's polity, especially the ISI, the possibility of a more rational neighbourhood policy looks unlikely. The enormous resources available to the Pakistan military cannot be justified without an enemy; the army needs an enemy to keep its power. On the rare occasion when candid conversations could be held with local friends, one heard the Pakistanis question the need for such a large and powerful army!

Will Pakistan be able to emerge out of the vicious cycle of debt, low tax collection, and poor governance and economy, caused mainly by military dominance, leading to impoverishment of its people? With increasing poverty, 'jihadists' can expect greater availability of cannon fodder churned out by madrassas, adding to the widespread radicalization of its population.

How long can Pakistan continue to slide down this downward slope before it falls over the precipice? What would that abyss look like? The instability in Afghanistan led to the creation of refugee camps on the Pakistani side,[35] with over 3.7 million Afghans fleeing Taliban rule. Where will the Pakistanis seek refuge, if the country falls into the abyss—Afghanistan, Iran or India? Pakistan's elite, including its politicians and powerful military, need to seriously ponder over the fate of the country if radical change is not made.

---

[35] 1,316,257 Registered Afghan Refugees in Pakistan, UNHCR, 31 December 2022, data.unhcr.org.

These questions are of great import to India. Instability and chaos across India's borders would have far-reaching implications for India's economy, polity and society. It is not just a truism to say that a stable and secure Pakistan is in India's enlightened interest.

Acknowledgements

I am not a writer. This is my first attempt at writing a book.

My friend Surina Narula, MBE, co-founder of the DSC prize for South Asian literature, the Jaipur Literature Festival and the Consortium for Street Children, was kind enough to go through the first few thousand words. Her frank and honest inputs helped me develop a narrative without getting overwhelmed by the background information that the diplomat in me wanted to include. I thank Surina for patiently reading through the first draft.

I got lost in the narrative after writing about a third of the book. I started work on another book and all but abandoned this one. The book was restarted in early 2022 when I met writer Javed Akhtar. His interest in my experience of living in Islamabad, followed by his words, 'And this is how, slowly, the narrative emerges,' made me take another look at the abandoned book. Suddenly, it all became clear after making a few changes to the structure of the book. I thank him for his encouraging and inspiring words.

Among the many historic developments that we lived through during our three years in Islamabad, perhaps the most impactful was Ghanashyam's visit to Kandahar after the hijacked flight IC 814 landed there. Friends continue to ask him to narrate his experience of going to the Taliban's Afghanistan. Over the years, he narrated several incidents from those days, but I could not have written about his experiences, even if I interviewed him. I am grateful that he agreed to write a separate chapter on the momentous days that he spent in Kandahar, without which the book would have remained incomplete.

Most of the book was written during the Covid-19 pandemic, when access to libraries was unavailable. The Internet became my accomplice in the writing of this book. My thanks to modern technology and the different tools that help us access information in the modern world.

I thank all the writers and journalists quoted and cited in the book. It is with deep respect and gratitude that I acknowledge their contribution in my journey of rediscovering Pakistan.

I am grateful to Penguin Random House India, especially Manasi Subramaniam, the editor who reviewed the book, for publishing a first book by an unknown writer. I also thank the entire team at Penguin Random House India for going through the book multiple times with me, especially Manali Das.

As I wrote about our days in Islamabad, I realized once again that I and Ghanashyam were not the only people affected by the struggle. Our children were intimately affected by the experience of living in Islamabad, especially during difficult times. They never told us of their traumas and struggles, even though they would have felt the strain when their parents were busy elsewhere. Some of their struggles are covered briefly in the book.

I thank everyone who helped me on my journey. My parents, Pushpa and late R.D. Shukla, sisters Prachi Sinha and Gunjan

Sharma for always being the supportive family without whom no success can be achieved.

My husband, A.R. Ghanashyam, and sons, Anant and Aniket Ghanashyam, have been my backbone through easy and difficult times. I could always depend on them to support and assist me. Without their steadfast support, I could never have achieved my potential.

Scan QR code to access the
Penguin Random House India website